Mapping the Path to 21st Century Healthcare

The Ten Transitions Workbook

Scott Goodwin

CRC Press is an imprint of the
Taylor & Francis Group, an **informa** business

A PRODUCTIVITY PRESS BOOK

CRC Press
Taylor & Francis Group
6000 Broken Sound Parkway NW, Suite 300
Boca Raton, FL 33487-2742

© 2016 by Scott Goodwin
CRC Press is an imprint of Taylor & Francis Group, an Informa business

No claim to original U.S. Government works

Printed on acid-free paper
Version Date: 20150820

International Standard Book Number-13: 978-1-4987-2686-3 (Paperback)

This book contains information obtained from authentic and highly regarded sources. Reasonable efforts have been made to publish reliable data and information, but the author and publisher cannot assume responsibility for the validity of all materials or the consequences of their use. The authors and publishers have attempted to trace the copyright holders of all material reproduced in this publication and apologize to copyright holders if permission to publish in this form has not been obtained. If any copyright material has not been acknowledged please write and let us know so we may rectify in any future reprint.

Except as permitted under U.S. Copyright Law, no part of this book may be reprinted, reproduced, transmitted, or utilized in any form by any electronic, mechanical, or other means, now known or hereafter invented, including photocopying, microfilming, and recording, or in any information storage or retrieval system, without written permission from the publishers.

For permission to photocopy or use material electronically from this work, please access www.copyright.com (http://www.copyright.com/) or contact the Copyright Clearance Center, Inc. (CCC), 222 Rosewood Drive, Danvers, MA 01923, 978-750-8400. CCC is a not-for-profit organization that provides licenses and registration for a variety of users. For organizations that have been granted a photocopy license by the CCC, a separate system of payment has been arranged.

Trademark Notice: Product or corporate names may be trademarks or registered trademarks, and are used only for identification and explanation without intent to infringe.

Visit the Taylor & Francis Web site at
http://www.taylorandfrancis.com

and the CRC Press Web site at
http://www.crcpress.com

To God for His grace to me in my Lord and Savior, Jesus Christ,

and

to my wife, BJ, for her love and support through the years

Contents

Author vii

Introduction ix

**SECTION I   THE GUIDE TO MAPPING THE PATH
TO 21ST CENTURY HEALTHCARE**

1   Understanding American Healthcare Development 3

2   Seeing the Path Ahead for American Healthcare 7

SECTION II   AMERICAN HEALTHCARE DEVELOPMENT

3   20th Century American Healthcare 13

4   American Healthcare Industrialization 21

5   21st Century American Healthcare 33

SECTION III   PREPARING TO TRANSITION TO 21ST CENTURY HEALTHCARE

6   Industrialization: Preparing to Transition 43

7   Industrialization Assessment 51

**SECTION IV   MAPPING YOUR ORGANIZATION'S
TRANSITION TO 21ST CENTURY HEALTHCARE**

8   Transition Groups: Organizational, Process, and Cultural 61

9   Transition Categories and Characteristics 65

10 Transition Assessment Tools 71

SECTION V   MAPPING THE TEN TRANSITIONS

11 Organizational Transition: Structure—Hierarchy to Complex
System 77
   20th Century Hierarchy 79
   21st Century Complex System 82

v

vi ■ *Contents*

12 Organizational Transition: Relationship—Transactional to Emergent **87**
20th Century Transactional Relationship 89
21st Century Emergent Relationship 91

13 Organizational Transition: Leadership—Control to Trust **97**
20th Century Control 98
21st Century Trust 101

14 Organizational Transition: Innovation—Centralized to Adaptive **105**
20th Century Centralized Innovation 106
21st Century Adaptive Innovation 109

15 Process Transition: Production Method—Craftsman to Multidisciplinary Teams **115**
20th Century Craftsman Production 116
21st Century Multidisciplinary Team Production 119

16 Process Transition: Delivery System—Hospital to Continuum of Care **123**
20th Century Hospital Delivery System 124
21st Century Continuum of Care Delivery System 127

17 Process Transition: Information System—Isolation to Network **131**
20th Century Information System Isolation 132
21st Century Information System Network 135

18 Process Transition: Financial—Fee-for-Service to Consumer Health Financing **139**
20th Century Fee-for-Service 140
21st Century Consumer Health Financing 143

19 Cultural Transition: Professional—Autonomy to Integration **149**
20th Century Professional Autonomy 151
21st Century Professional Integration 154

20 Cultural Transition: Metaphor—Scientific Machine to Complex Adaptive System **159**
20th Century Scientific Machine 161
21st Century Healthcare Complex Adaptive System 164

SECTION VI FOLLOWING THE MAP TO 21ST CENTURY HEALTHCARE

21 Signposts and Motivation for the Journey **171**

22 Next Steps **175**

References **177**

Index **181**

Author

Scott Goodwin, MBA, D.A., CPHQ, LSSBB, has more than 20 years' experience as a healthcare quality professional that includes hospital senior quality leadership positions and quality consulting with multiple hospitals. He is currently the owner/chief innovation officer for AWLG Healthcare Consulting, LLC. Since 2013, he has been an adjunct professor at New England College in Henniker, New Hampshire, where he teaches healthcare quality and Lean and organizational ethics. In 2014, he received the Innovator's Award from the New Hampshire Foundation for Healthy Communities, which celebrates extraordinary ingenuity, creativity, and skill in improving health and healthcare access, delivery, or quality. Over the past 10 years, he has studied the influences shaping American healthcare organizations and healthcare quality improvement. As a result of his studies in these areas, he determined that American healthcare is progressing from its current 20th century phase to the 21st century phase by passing through a period of industrialization and a series of ten transitions. He currently assists healthcare organizations in recognizing these phases within their own operations and in supporting them as they map their transitions to 21st century healthcare. He is the author of *Transition to 21st Century Healthcare: A Guide for Leaders and Quality Professionals* (CRC Press, 2015).

Introduction

Everyone involved in American healthcare today wonders what the future will be like. The multitude and magnitude of the changes affecting this vital part of American life create a blur that seems designed to resist any attempt to see what lies ahead. While acknowledging the inherent dangers in predicting the future of healthcare in America, this book offers eyeglasses to see the reference points and the tools to map the path that leads to that future. The endpoint in the journey has not appeared yet because it is still being created. Recognizing the signs from the past and following the paths that lead to the future offer the best hope for organizations seeking to move forward on the journey.

The book *Transition to 21st Century Healthcare: A Guide for Leaders and Quality Professionals* (CRC Press, 2015) provided a high-level view of American healthcare as transitioning through a period of industrialization, breaking down the familiar but fading structures of 20th century healthcare and paving the way for the rapidly emerging but unfamiliar 21st century healthcare. A part of this view of the overall transitional state of American healthcare included initial guidance in assessing the status of healthcare organizations relative to the ten transitions that appear out of the conflict between industrialization and 20th century healthcare. This book offers a review of the fundamentals of the transitional structure presented in the first book but shifts the focus to a much more intensive discussion of industrialization, the ten transitions, and the way to use these transitions to create a vision to move healthcare organizations into the future.

For healthcare organizations, the term "transition" has become a familiar expression today that points to passage or movement from one state, stage, or place to another (Merriam-Webster Online Dictionary). Recognizing that the seemingly stable institutions of the past no longer characterize the nature of healthcare in America today opens the way to recognizing that transitions define the path to the evolving future of healthcare. This future offers hope for healthcare to become the service that takes care of patient–customers in all aspects of their lives rather than a healthcare production industry built on costly hospital-based technology, questionable quality, and limited options. By thinking in terms of transitions, the perspective shifts from the fading fortresses of healthcare's past to the natural state of healthcare as a continuously evolving complex system serving the changing needs of patient–customers through innovative processes that adapt to deliver higher quality at a lower cost.

Section I, The Guide to Mapping the Path to 21st Century Healthcare, offers an introduction to the concepts that underlie the structure and methodology of the book. It provides the rationale for viewing the development of American healthcare through the three metaphors of 20th century healthcare, industrialization, and 21st century healthcare as points of reference for understanding and recognizing the path to the future. Building on this structure, it points to the future of healthcare as arising out of the unanticipated results of applying industrial quality to a healthcare industry still based in the 20th century. This industrialization process breaks down the structures, values, and traditions of the past and leads to the emergence of ten transitions that serve as generative metaphors in the creation of the new vision of healthcare that leads into the future.

Section II, American Healthcare Development, offers a historical view of American healthcare that highlights the fundamental distinctions between 20th and 21st century healthcare and the role of industrialization in the transition from one century to the other. Though not intended to be comprehensive, it draws on the key aspects of American healthcare history that led to industrialization and the appearance of the transitions to 21st century healthcare. Recognizing the three developmental periods in American healthcare and the dynamics that shape them leads to the next steps of understanding the industrialization of healthcare.

Section III, Preparing to Transition to 21st Century Healthcare, narrows the focus to the vital role that industrialization plays in revealing the transitions from 20th to 21st century healthcare. Industrialization in the form of industrial quality and industrial operational concepts conflicts with the assumptions that constitute 20th century healthcare. As industrialization progresses, it breaks down the vestiges of the 20th century that remain within healthcare organizations. This leads to the formation of the ten transitions as the initial images of 21st century healthcare appear, and the final traces of 20th century healthcare that no longer fit begin to fade. This section explains the significance of fully implementing industrialization in all areas of healthcare organizations as the means for initiating the transition to 21st century healthcare. Without it, the transitions may not be recognized, and organizations may fail to progress toward the future.

Section IV, Mapping Your Organization's Transition to 21st Century Healthcare, presents the structure of the transitions. This section describes the groups of transitions and the categories and characteristics that form the transitions. Within each transition, a continuum exists that begins with a category or an important aspect of healthcare organizations from the 20th century and ends with a category that converts that 20th century aspect of healthcare into a vision or image of how it will be in the 21st century. Moving from the 20th to 21st century end of the continuum is the basis for the transition, and this movement appears as the characteristics of organizations change through transitions. This section offers tools to assess progress through the transitions and guidance in recognizing the characteristics of 20th and 21st century healthcare.

Section V, Mapping the Ten Transitions, offers an in-depth look within each of the ten transitions and explains how they provide an understanding of the movement of healthcare from the 20th to 21st century. Understanding the ten transitions by contrasting the categories reflecting 20th century healthcare and the categories that envision 21st century healthcare pulls back the curtain to reveal the past that shaped much of healthcare today and the future that incorporates its highest aspirations as expressed within healthcare organizations. The broad sweep of this section incorporates the four organizational transitions, the four process transitions, and the two cultural transitions. Finally, Section VI, Following the Map to 21st Century Healthcare, closes the book with an explanation of the value of the generative or guiding and motivating metaphors in the transitions formed through the contrast between the 20th and 21st century categories. With the metaphors as motivation, the final section encourages healthcare organizations to use the tools and to begin their intentional journey to 21st century healthcare.

It may be helpful to think of this book as eyeglasses with three lenses like trifocals. As you put on these glasses, they make the blurred, chaotic images of healthcare in America clearer by enabling you to see it through the metaphors. As you look through one focus on the glasses, you are able to see 20th century healthcare and the important aspects that shaped healthcare during that period and that continue today. Shifting your focus to the next lens shows you the elements of industrialization that are currently working their way through American healthcare and creating the environment that brings out the ten transitions. Finally, as you look up through the glasses, you are able to focus on the 21st century, and the future images created by the ten transitions appear.

The terms "leader," "leadership," and "position power or positional power" are important in understanding organizational changes in healthcare between the 20th and 21st centuries. The definition for leader in this book is "someone who leads" (Merriam-Webster Online Dictionary) as a simple way of indicating that it may be what someone does (functional) or what someone is. "Position power" and "positional power" in this book refer to "authority and influence bestowed by a position or office on whoever is filling or occupying it" (BusinessDictionary.com). "Manager" and "management" or the specific title (e.g., CEO) will refer to "someone who is in charge of a business or department" (Merriam-Webster Online Dictionary) by the position that they hold. "Administrator" is often used to designate the top management position in a hospital and "administration" is used as a term for the top management of a hospital. In the leadership transition, an additional perspective on leadership referred to as "relational leadership" will be presented (Uhl-Bien 2006).

As a new set of glasses, this workbook offers you a new perspective on American healthcare that gives you greater insight into what is happening and helps you to see the paths that lead to the future. Using the new trifocal perspectives, you can understand the origins and the transitions occurring in American healthcare and begin to participate in the realization of the 21st century healthcare that we all aspire to achieve. This workbook serves to focus your attention on those areas of healthcare and healthcare organizations that are most useful for you to consider for your own understanding of healthcare and for the work of helping healthcare organizations to progress into the 21st century. Please put on your glasses, and join me as we map the path to the future of American healthcare.

Scott Goodwin

THE GUIDE TO MAPPING THE PATH TO 21ST CENTURY HEALTHCARE

1

Chapter 1

Understanding American Healthcare Development

It may surprise you, but making sense of American healthcare today requires metaphors. You probably noted in the title of the book terms like "mapping," "path," and "21st century." These are metaphors. Taking these familiar terms that usually refer to people finding their way and applying them to healthcare create a new perspective for you. As you looked at the title, you may have read "healthcare," but you also read "mapping" and "path," which you do not usually associate with healthcare. The familiar images of maps and paths brought to mind past experiences or thoughts of yourself looking at maps to try to find the path to a destination, and you applied them as metaphors to 21st century healthcare. You applied your sense of mapping and paths and created a mental image that made sense to you. That is essentially how metaphors work to help us interpret our world and healthcare. Now that you know what metaphors are—the application of familiar words, concepts, and images to something else that is unrelated in order to use that familiarity to interpret and create new understanding (Lakoff and Johnson 1980; Goodwin 2013)—you are ready to use them to explore the map of healthcare and to find the path to the future.

In this book, as in my previous book, an important metaphor is the word "transition" applied to organizations so you can visualize changing over time from one state to another. By using the word "transition" as denoting change over time, it brings to mind images of other things that change over time such as children or plants, and you apply those images to the idea of healthcare organizations. Transition in this case, then, refers to the development of American healthcare from one state to another.

In the case of the transition of healthcare organizations, it starts in the time roughly between 1900 and 1999 that we commonly call the "20th century." The end of this particular transition is sometime in the future that falls within the period we can call the "21st century" or prior to January 1, 2100. In your mind, then, you can imagine healthcare organizations as transitioning or changing between these two periods. To simplify it, when I refer to "20th century healthcare," I am referring to healthcare organizations with characteristics common in the 20th century. When I refer to "21st century healthcare," I am referring to healthcare organizations as they will be in the future. These metaphors help us to talk about healthcare because they enable us to think about large, complex things using simple phrases that we understand.

I realize that using a phrase like "20th century" to talk about organizations that were part of that century or that reflect characteristics of that century combines a multitude of important and unique things under a common phrase. This is part of the value and danger of metaphors. By applying a familiar expression like "20th century" to healthcare organizations, it brings to mind the nature and characteristics of healthcare organizations during the period without having to name all those characteristics individually. This makes it much easier to talk about the nature of organizations in that period. At the same time, it lumps many things from the period together that are very different. To help with this possibility, I provided specific chapters on 20th and 21st century healthcare to clarify the particular aspects of each century's healthcare that the metaphor encompasses.

Another important part of using the familiar 20th century as a metaphor for healthcare during that period and 21st century as the metaphor for healthcare in the future is the way that phrase makes you feel and gives you a sense of direction. You may have had personal experiences that occurred in the 20th century that come to mind when you think of that period. Some of those memories may be about healthcare. You may remember a particular physician who managed your healthcare as part of a close personal relationship. The image of a personal relationship with an individual physician who treated you in the office or hospital and perhaps came to your home represents the image many people associate with American healthcare in the 20th century. By using 20th century healthcare as a metaphor, images like this may come to your mind and help you to understand the changes occurring in healthcare in a richer way.

In the same way, by using the image of 21st century healthcare, different feelings and mental images come to mind. Though the future is unknown in a total sense, you can project current trends into the mists ahead and see what may be likely. Most of us would agree that the close personal relationship with an individual physician that characterized the 20th century is not likely to be the same for the 21st century. In place of the individual physician relationship of the past, you may associate a recent healthcare experience with new technology and with many different types of professionals managing your care as 21st century healthcare.

By placing the two metaphors of 20th and 21st century healthcare side by side in this book, the metaphors enable you to begin to recognize how they are different. Through your experiences that occurred during the two periods, you may also have feelings and memories that help to shape your understanding of the differences. You also have a strong sense of the direction of healthcare. You see 20th century healthcare as the past and what remains of it as old or fading. You recognize 21st century healthcare as the future. By placing these two metaphors together, you can feel the past slipping away and the pull to the future, and you experience in your mind the transition of American healthcare as personal and real.

Once you have in your mind the sense of the transition of American healthcare from the 20th to 21st century, there is one other metaphor that helps to make this transition meaningful by answering the question "why." When you see changes around you, you try to figure out why the changes occurred. Changes such as transitions usually happen because something sets them in motion. The word "industrialization" will serve as the metaphor for influences that set the transition of American healthcare in motion and to describe the period in which it influenced healthcare. As you think about industrialization, you probably go back in your mind to your classes in school and pictures of iron blast furnaces glowing in dark factories with chimneys belching smoke. Placing those images of the Industrial Revolution in the midst of healthcare images can be startling and disorienting. Though the metaphor of industrialization as applied to healthcare is not about iron furnaces, your sense of disorientation in trying to apply it to healthcare is actually useful to help you understand how industrialization is the source of the transition between 20th and 21st century healthcare.

If you think of the 20th century as the past and the 21st century as the future of healthcare, the industrialization period is happening now. Beginning in the 1980s and continuing into the near future, industrialization serves as the reason that 20th century healthcare is breaking down and fading away, and 21st century healthcare is taking shape and becoming clearer. This metaphor of industrialization signifies the introduction into American healthcare of the concepts and methods that transformed American industry in the 1980s and 1990s. In simple terms, this metaphor is about changes in American healthcare produced by introducing industrial techniques for measuring and improving quality and for reducing costs. The motivation for introducing industrial quality methods into healthcare resulted initially from the high costs of healthcare and secondarily from questions about quality. In the 1980s, questions about costs drew blank stares from American healthcare, and questions about quality drew loud protests. No one seemed to have answers. Since American industry found ways to reduce costs and improve quality to compete with Japan in the 1990s, the answers from industry became the route for the industrialization of healthcare that continues today.

The introduction of industrialization into healthcare came only after no other options appeared, and costs continued to rise to the point that people were willing to try whatever might work. By introducing industrialization into healthcare, however, the essential nature of American healthcare as it developed in the 20th century began to change. Though it is still in its early stages, industrialization breaks down the basic assumptions underlying 20th century healthcare because they are inconsistent with industrial methods. To achieve cost reductions and to improve quality, the structures, practices, and values of 20th century healthcare must change. Since 20th century healthcare remains the metaphor for most of American healthcare, this represents a significant change and the reason for the transition to 21st century healthcare. As industrialization advances in healthcare organizations across America and breaks down the essential structures of 20th century healthcare, it sets in motion the transition to 21st century healthcare.

The metaphors of 20th century healthcare, industrialization, and 21st century healthcare serve to define the basic structure for understanding what is happening in American healthcare as it transitions from the 20th to 21st century. In Chapter 2, the focus shifts to the important active role of metaphors in the transition process. Using the three period metaphors already discussed as contexts, other metaphors serve to motivate and guide healthcare organizations as they seek to make the transition. They map the path to the future by describing specific changes in organizations as they move through the transition and work to achieve the vision of 21st century healthcare that is just beginning to appear.

Chapter 2

Seeing the Path Ahead
for American Healthcare

Making the changes required to become a 21st century healthcare organization requires metaphors that provide the images or vision of what this looks like to motivate and guide the changes (Morgan 1993, 2006; Goodwin 2013). For most organizations, the current environment in healthcare is changing so fast that they rarely have time to consider something as seemingly remote as a distant concept of 21st century healthcare. In reality, however, the industrialization of healthcare occurring now portends the arrival of 21st century healthcare, and many organizations may not be ready for it. Choosing not to be ready when the future arrives can be an organization-ending decision.

Mapping the path to 21st century healthcare has become more difficult because of all the noise, activity, and competing perspectives that create confusion, disorientation, and an inability to see which paths to take. Healthcare incorporates so many facets of life in America that the complexity overwhelms most attempts to try to understand what is happening or where to go. Industrialization serves as the catalyst for the transition of American healthcare from the 20th to 21st century and offers a focal point for discovering the way forward in healthcare.

Industrialization did not occur as part of a great plan to improve healthcare. The infusion of industrial quality and concepts into healthcare occurred because there were no other options for dealing with the costs and quality issues of healthcare. With industrialization active in healthcare and spreading, the effects of this treatment are more extensive and more transformative than many anticipated. Industrialization breaks down 20th century American healthcare by challenging the assumptions that underlie it as inconsistent with industrial concepts and processes. As industrialization challenges and replaces the traditions, practices, and values of 20th century healthcare, specific areas in healthcare organizations begin to transition to another state. Using these transition areas as guides enables healthcare organizations to identify the paths to the future and to begin to see the images of what that future will be.

Metaphors offer the means for translating the transformation of 20th century healthcare through industrialization into meaningful visions of the key areas of change that create the path to the future. By framing the changes occurring in healthcare as ten transitions, this book offers organizations a way to focus on the key aspects of change and provides the means for assessing their own progress toward the future. The ten transitions use metaphors to frame the movement between the current states of healthcare organizations and what they will be like in the future.

The starting point for each of the transitions is a key aspect of 20th century healthcare. The destination for each transition is the same aspect as it may be in 21st century healthcare. These key aspects or categories for each century are metaphors that depict the aspect as it existed in organizations in the particular century. For example, the first transition is organizational structure. The 20th century category for organizational structure is hierarchy. Hierarchy is a metaphor for organizations that organize in a vertical bureaucracy with positions of power at the top of the hierarchy and the rest reporting to them. The 21st century category for organizational structure is a complex system. A complex system is a metaphor for organizations that consist of many individuals connected through information systems that coordinate their activities as semi-independent agents based on common values and mission.

The importance of the ten transitions is that they provide a sense of direction for organizations working to understand what is happening to them and where they are going in the future. Healthcare leaders and organizations often lack consensus on the direction of healthcare or their organizations, and this prevents many organizations from moving forward. Using the structure of the transitions, the sense of direction comes from the 20th century metaphor as clearly designating the past and the 21st century metaphor clearly designating the future. By placing these metaphors side by side, the effect is to create a generative metaphor (Schön 1979; Barrett and Cooperrider 1990; Goodwin 2013). Generative metaphors present a duality in which the names of the metaphors offer a clear sense of the relationship of the two. In this case, the 20th and 21st century metaphors clearly designate the past and the future. This comparison offers a sense of the direction of the transition of healthcare from the past to the future.

This generative metaphor effect continues with the categories. As illustrated above, the organizational structure transition aligns the category of hierarchy with the 20th century. The category of complex system aligns with the 21st century. The structure of the transitions displays the metaphors of the 20th and 21st century and the categories for each century side by side. This configuration makes the direction of the transition clear. By using these metaphors arranged in these formats, the transitions serve to create generative metaphors pointing to the future to enable organizations to build consensus on the direction forward and to motivate employees to pursue the goal of achieving 21st century healthcare. The ten transitions as generative metaphors unite people in organizations by encouraging consensus that supports organizational change and a common sense of direction.

Through this structure of the duality of generative metaphors and specific categories of changes, the transitions reduce the complexity of healthcare to a relationship between the 20th and 21st century and between two representative categories. Reflecting on the 20th century images as the past that is fading and recognizing the 21st century as the future that is coming into view, organizations gain the direction they need to build the future. In this way, the transitions serve as generative metaphors because they result in a sense of direction that can guide and motivate organizations in their efforts to achieve 21st century healthcare. The power of the generative metaphor lies in the creation of a new sense of knowing what to do and where to go (Schön 1979).

Specific chapters in the book describe in detail the ten transitions and the use of the generative metaphors. The transition assessment charts use the structure of the centuries and the categories to guide organizations in identifying specific characteristics that align with that century and the category. Once organizations have identified the characteristics in their own organizations that reflect the 20th and 21st century category, they can assess whether they are progressing toward the goal of 21st century healthcare or are remaining attached to the past. With this insight and the awareness of the importance of preparing for the future, the organization can strengthen the consensus on the path ahead for achieving 21st century healthcare.

AMERICAN HEALTHCARE DEVELOPMENT

Chapter 3

20th Century American Healthcare

As you think about your own experiences in healthcare and healthcare organizations, you may be like many Americans today who characterize healthcare as broken, fragmented, and irreparable. Using your newly acquired glasses with special lenses, however, you have the ability to see the reality of American healthcare as transitioning through clearly identifiable stages of development. This provides you with insights into why it functions the way it does and what it will look like in the future. You are now prepared to see the three developmental periods for American healthcare as two centuries and an intermediate period: 20th century healthcare, 21st century healthcare, and a period between and overlapping the centuries that can be described as a period of industrialization. The first developmental period is the 20th century encompassing the period between 1900 and 1999. During this century, aspects of healthcare were developed that ultimately led to the industrialization phase that followed. Healthcare entered a period of industrialization beginning in the 1980s and continues at the current time. Industrialization challenges 20th century healthcare in the way healthcare understands itself and operates, and this creates dramatic differences between the past and the future. Finally, 21st century healthcare has begun but only exists today in its earliest forms. The actual start date may not be discernible until some years in the future. The 21st century period represents American healthcare as it emerges out of the industrialization phase and begins to demonstrate very different characteristics because of the interaction between 20th century healthcare and industrialization (Goodwin 2015).

Focusing initially on the 20th century offers a developmental perspective on American healthcare that identifies four key elements during this period that prepared the way for the industrialization phase that follows. In describing 20th century healthcare, the four aspects that are important to the development of the industrialization phase are professionalization of physicians, emergence of technology exemplified by the hospital, the central role of the paper medical record in shaping healthcare organizational processes, and, finally, insurance as the basis for payment for healthcare services. Each of these was developed in American healthcare during the 20th century and contributed to the eventual introduction of industrialization into healthcare.

It may seem simplistic to think of reducing 20th century healthcare down to four essential aspects, but this actually makes sense within the context of the unique character of healthcare. The basic activities of healthcare occur thousands of times a day in hospitals, doctor's offices, clinics, laboratories, and other sites. Even the smallest change in the way healthcare operates or functions when it is widely communicated becomes transformative. This is why the four elements that are fundamental to 20th century healthcare can provide the basis for understanding healthcare's development and its current transitional processes (Goodwin 2015).

With new glasses firmly in place and looking through the lenses of the 20th century, look at your healthcare experiences and the organizations you are familiar with, and consider the four elements as they appear to you beginning with the central role of the physician in 20th century healthcare.

It would be difficult to miss the 20th century physician as a white-coated male or female who is the central figure in any healthcare organization but particularly the hospital. Everyone you see is focused on this individual and looking to this person for information and direction. Writing orders by hand in the medical record in a script that may be difficult to decipher and documenting notes on the patients he/she has seen, the physician creates the processes of care through his/her orders and notes. Waiting for orders is a typical part of the care process because nothing happens apart from the orders. The only questions concerning the orders by the physician are for clarification since the physician is the only person licensed by the state medical board and privileged by the hospital medical staff to write orders. Nurses taking care of the patients quickly read the orders, and the chain of communication moves from the nursing station on the patient care unit to the pharmacy for medications or to the laboratory for specimens or to radiology for testing.

There is no discussion about the costs resulting from the orders. Whether the patient's care is $500 or $1 million, the individual physician's order drives the economic as well as clinical process. The hospital operates on the orders of the physician. They are the fuel if you consider a hospital similar to a production facility. All of the technology, support staff, and care resources await the physician's orders to go into motion.

The patient is not a part of the physician's orders except to the expected compliance in supplying information or following instructions. Enculturation of patients to defer to white coats and physicians begins early in life, and patients understand that the physician knows what is best for them, and their life and health depend on following the physician's orders. The nursing staff assures noncompliant patients that the physician knows what he/she is doing, and the patient's best hope for recovery lies in agreeing to whatever the physician orders.

The handwritten notes that the physician documents in the paper medical chart become the basis for interpretation of the patient's condition and for the next steps in the care process. The notes serve as the basis not only for the care of the patient but also for the charges that the hospital will send to the insurance company, if the patient is insured, or to the patient if there is no insurance. Coders in the hospital carefully review all the information that the physician documents and use them to develop the charges for the patient's care. For many agencies and payers, only the physician's orders and notes represent the true status of the patient and the description of the services rendered during the hospital stay.

Through your special lenses for seeing 20th century healthcare, you see the physician in a leadership role in the medical staff. The medical staff ostensibly reports to the board of the hospital, but it is hard to miss the significant organizational influence that the medical staff exerts as it conducts its business. Members of the medical staff elect their own officers who represent them to the administration and board of the hospital. Obtaining privileges at the hospital requires the medical staff review of a physician's credentials and a vote of approval of the medical executive committee and board. When they become members of the medical staff, physicians agree to abide by the medical staff bylaws, rules, and regulations. Only those policies implemented by the hospital and approved by the medical staff apply to the members. In all regards, however, the licensure of the physician serves as the basis for making decisions about the care of patients, and only a peer physician who has the credentials can evaluate the practice of another member of the medical staff.

As you look at the physician with your 20th century vision, you see this individual in meetings with hospital administration and in the community. Wherever the physician appears, the conversation and flow of activities change based on the physician's comments and demeanor. The ability of the physician to control resources not only in terms of clinical care but also in terms of operations of the hospital and the way businesses operate in the community translates into enormous economic power and influence at all levels of the community. Physician schedules and preferences shape hospital workflows and processes. Hospitals design and adapt waiting rooms, support staff, office space, and equipment around individual physicians.

As you observe the 20th century physician through your new glasses, you are able to see the unique role of this individual and this profession in American healthcare during this period. You see that the design and operation of American healthcare in all its dimensions from the individual order written by hand in the medical record to the whispered advice to high officials to reject national health insurance were shaped by professional physicians in the 20th century. You are, therefore, not surprised as you glance through the industrialization portion of your glasses and recognize the physician as the center of the controversy over the next phase of American healthcare development (Starr 1982).

Shifting your focus from the physician to the world he/she commands, you recognize the hospital of the 20th century. You remember that healthcare started out in the home as the physician came to see the patients who could pay for services, and the family took care of the ill and injured after the physician left. Only the poor who were deemed worthy could receive care in the hospital. With the advent of new technology in the form of anesthesia, aseptic surgery, x-rays, and laboratories, physicians found that the cost and difficulty of setting up equipment in homes required that this technology be delivered in its own unique facility (Howell 1995). With no other appropriate locations available, the technology appeared in the hospital as physicians encouraged the governing board to purchase, staff, and operate these new marvels of engineering and science, and the physicians provided the patients. As new technology produced better outcomes, physicians persuaded their patients to gradually move from their homes to the hospital. In this way, technology not only transformed the care process but also led to the centrality of the hospital as the site and source of care. The transition from home to hospital represents a significant change in healthcare in the 20th century that leads to serious repercussions in the future (Rosenberg 1987).

Once the technology of healthcare found a home in the hospital, the hospital found itself, along with the physician, at the center of American healthcare throughout the 20th century. This partnership between physicians who ordered and controlled the technology and hospitals that purchased, operated, and maintained it characterized the American healthcare experience throughout the century. Building hospitals became the equivalent of delivering healthcare because physicians trained to practice medicine with hospitals needed the facilities, and state and federal funds built hospitals wherever the population reached certain levels in the middle of the 20th century (Rosenberg 1987).

As you look through your 20th century lenses, you recognize the operating rooms, radiology equipment, and laboratories as all familiar parts of the hospital of the period. The central role of the hospital as the place to obtain healthcare seems exactly right. The partnership of the physicians and the hospital typifies the delivery of healthcare, and all the services and physicians that patients need are associated with the hospital. As you survey the scene, there is nothing unusual in outpatients and inpatients side by side vying for the same equipment and waiting for the same tests in the hospital. Waiting rooms abound for people waiting for tests or results or to see the physician, and none of that seems unusual. There is no real sense of the hospital as only being for the very sick. You know that the very sick go to the hospital, but you recognize the hospital as a 20th century healthcare production facility for outpatients as well. Cost is not a consideration, and the technology to perform the testing is all at the hospital along with the specialists who perform the procedures and interpret the results.

Shifting your eyes up to the industrialization lenses, you are surprised to see fewer outpatients and inpatients in the holding areas and waiting rooms than from the 20th century perspective. Your focus shifts to outpatient facilities outside of the hospital, and you find that the waiting areas have more people. It is clear between the 20th century perspective and the industrialization view that hospitals lost some of their patients to outpatient facilities that were more convenient and less expensive. You begin to think that the industrialization process with its focus on cost, quality, and convenience of patients could lead to fewer patients in the hospital. The technology is the same, the environment is much friendlier, and the cost for the procedures is lower. You intend to remember that when you decide to do a deeper dive on industrialization.

Through your 20th century lenses, the paper medical record looks very familiar to you. It is like a chair, table, or any common article in the hospital. You watch the physician writing in the record, and it all looks the way healthcare is supposed to look in the hospital. Surely the medical record is not part of the problem that led to industrialization. The role of the medical record in the delivery of care represents an important aspect of 20th century healthcare that only recently began to change. The hospital medical record began as the private notes of the physician making rounds in the hospital or written orders left for hospital staff. Over time, the role of the handwritten orders and the notes about patients evolved to become the official documentation of the patient's care. By 1919, the American College of Surgeons, as part of the Minimum Standards Program, required that "accurate and complete records are to be written for all patients, easily accessible with specific content" (American College of Surgeons 2006). It not only guided the care of the patient and the doctor's assessment of the patient's progress, but also, as paying patients increased in the hospital, it became the basis for hospital charges to the patient. Long after most industries, particularly industries as technology heavy as healthcare, moved to computer information systems, healthcare refused to give up its handwritten paper medical record. The continuance of the medical record at the insistence in many cases of the physician reaffirmed the preeminence of the physician in the hospital and the principal defenders of the status quo.

Though the paper medical records seem perfectly normal in your 20th century lenses, you know that it is an iconic image of the paradox of American healthcare. The significance of the paper medical record in the hospital lies in its effect on the workflows and the structure of hospital clinical processes. Vital patient information needed by everyone involved in the care of patients rests in the single paper medical record. The inability of the staff to access the record or to find it in certain cases and to be able to interpret the physician's handwriting significantly affected the delivery of care to patients. The handwritten medical record served as a cornerstone of the workflow of the individual physician and represented the ability of professional staff in many instances to retain less efficient work processes due to personal preference or simply lack of interest in changes.

As you turn your head and look through your industrialization lenses, you become aware of the presence of computers everywhere you look in healthcare facilities. You see physicians sitting at terminals and typing on keyboards. This represented a significant shift from the defense of the paper medical record to the proliferation of computers and electronic medical records as part of governmental incentives and efforts to reduce injuries and errors. Workflows changed painfully with computers, but they expanded the ability of more people to access information and to be engaged in the care of the patients. Multiple disciplines accessing the patient's medical record simultaneously promoted the capability for team interactions and sharing information. You can tell that this new connectivity and communication offer real advantages for the future.

Looking through your 20th century lenses, the use of insurance to pay for healthcare seems very familiar. Insurance as a means for paying for physician and hospital care is a notable characteristic of 20th century American healthcare and had always been a part of your experience.

With the hospital as the home for healthcare technology, physicians began to encourage their patients to go to the hospital for care. The costs of hospital care rose as the cost of technology increased, and patients struggled to find the means to pay for the care that now seemed very attractive. This became particularly acute during the Depression era of the 1930s, and patients needed new ways of managing payments. The American entrepreneurial spirit rescued healthcare with the idea of prepayments for hospital services to guarantee the availability of services in the event of illness or injury. This payment model supported the view of hospital services as a routine part of healthcare and prepayment as an acceptable way to finance it. The move from the prepayment of hospital services to healthcare insurance represented a reasonable progression also supported by the American entrepreneurial drive. Individuals and families received hospital insurance coverage as a benefit of employment and did not directly pay for hospital care or have to worry about shopping for services they could afford. Hospitals, insurers, and employers worked it all out (Thomasson 2003; Starr 2011).

As you observe the way healthcare functions in the 20th century through your special glasses, you see the relationship among hospitals, physicians, and employer-sponsored insurance as a very reasonable and smoothly operating system. Patients really have no worries as long as their employer-sponsored healthcare covers the services they need. The insurer, the hospital, and the physicians work out all the arrangements without ever requiring the patient to be involved in the discussions. The payment mechanism is a card that the patient shows like a credit card, but there is no bill later as the insurer pays the hospital or the physician. The patient usually has no idea what the costs are for the services or how much each provider is paid. You also see many people who do not have insurance at work having difficulty paying for care and many who were unable to obtain insurance due to preexisting conditions (Stevens 1999). You also recall that it was only in 1965 that Medicare was implemented, and the elderly and the poor finally had access to healthcare insurance.

A quick glance through the industrialization lenses brings to light a new reality of high costs for healthcare that seem to increase continuously particularly for Medicare. Employers are reducing the insurance coverage they provide employees to reduce cost increases, and insurers are creating ever-smaller networks of providers to reduce costs. You notice patients asking about costs and shopping for cheaper healthcare as the most significant change between this new period and the 20th century. You find this puzzling because in the 20th century, the physician directed patients to the place where they should get care, and patients did not concern themselves about cost. With the new policies, the patient has become responsible for a significant portion of the cost, and shopping for cheaper prices has become a part of the healthcare process. Patients as paying customers appear to be a new role emerging out of the industrialization process as a means that employers and the government are using to reduce costs (Bernard 2014).

As you consider your experiences in looking at healthcare through the 20th century lenses of your special glasses, you recognize that the institutional stability of healthcare during the period covered over serious issues. Though the physicians and the hospital-based delivery system appeared to function well in meeting the needs of patients and the community, many of the structures and practices supporting healthcare carried within them problems that would contribute to the breakdown of the system.

The unique professional status of the physician meant that there were very few checks on the individual practitioner. Quality and costs were based on the prerogative of the individual physician with little oversight or even awareness by anyone else of the potential for problems. The physician's role in the hospital and in the community and ability to order services without regard for costs led to decisions about care based on personal preferences and practices that tended to produce excessive costs and lower quality.

The hospitals, like the physicians, established pricing and services that maximized revenue with little oversight related to costs or quality. As long as insurers paid for the costs of care, hospitals purchased new technology and used it whenever the physician ordered it without regard for frequency or costs. Hospitals acquired new technology to attract physicians and patients by publicizing the latest and greatest technology as the basis for high-quality care.

At the behest of physicians, the paper medical records lingered as the emblem of healthcare's resistance to changes in clinical process. This one document strengthened the position of the individual physician by reducing access to information to only what the physician documented by hand. This less efficient and potentially harmful form of documentation continued despite the availability of a better method for documenting care and sharing information. By limiting access to information, the paper record reduced the ability of hospital staff to coordinate care.

Finally, the insurance payment process sets in motion a variety of factors that ultimately led to the distortion of healthcare charges and payments and reduced the ability to link payment to actual costs. Arcane negotiations among insurers, physicians, and hospitals led to charges and payments unrelated to actual costs. Employers often paid higher rates as hospitals shifted costs within the charge-master to maximize reimbursement. Insurers limited access to services to reduce costs to employers.

Perhaps most symptomatic of the breakdown of the system was the lack of a true customer who actually received and paid for the service and looked for quality at a reasonable cost. Healthcare's cost and payment processes eliminated the patient as a true customer by obscuring the processes for setting pricing and eliminating any true alignment with costs. Patients had no access to the information about costs or charges and had to wait for the bill to arrive to know its total. It evolved as an artificial process negotiated at agreed-upon levels of payment with minimal relationship to a market reality.

In the 20th century, American healthcare achieved amazing progress that completely transformed the concept of healthcare for Americans. Physicians, hospitals, technology, and insurance all contributed to high-quality healthcare for a portion of the American people. In the four critical areas of physician professionalization, hospital technology, organizational communication, and insurance-based healthcare, however, American healthcare in the 20th century set in motion cultural, economic, and technological systems that produced high levels of complications, injury and death to patients, and limited access to care for millions and cost more than any other healthcare on earth. The successes did not outweigh the failures, and the result in the 1980s was the industrialization of American healthcare.

Chapter 4

American Healthcare Industrialization

At the end of the 20th century, a number of factors surprisingly pushed American healthcare in a new direction. This new direction called the "industrialization phase" of American healthcare appeared when the consensus in government and industry coalesced around the belief that costs could not continue rising at the same rate, and quality had to improve. The standard definition of industrialization as "conversion to the methods, aims, and ideals of industry" (dictionary.com) provides a useful starting point in understanding healthcare industrialization, but it misses an important element. Healthcare industrialization is the conversion to industrial *quality* methods, aims, and ideals. The significant difference is the emphasis on quality rather than simply duplicating manufacturing. The industrialization phase of healthcare described here focuses on the industrial quality movement that began in Japan following World War II and was developed in America in the 1980s following the failure of American mass production to compete with the higher quality coming out of Japan (Dobyns and Crawford-Mason 1991).

It is important to see healthcare industrialization as a phase of American healthcare development rather than to view it as a change to a permanent state. The industrialization phase of healthcare results from the disparity between 20th and 21st century American healthcare in efficiency, cost, and quality. Insulated from cultural and economic forces by professionalization, local practices, and federal regulation, 20th century American healthcare failed to adapt to the changing environment in America that developed during the 1970s and 1980s. As foreign competition and new quality methods in manufacturing and service industries created new standards, expectations, and efficiencies, American healthcare with its traditional methods of operation and management failed to adapt to this new environment. After minor attempts at change within healthcare, industrialization using the new quality concepts and methods became the only option for addressing the issues of cost and quality afflicting healthcare (IOM 2012).

21

Healthcare as a service industry did not anticipate industrialization. Most Americans and most of the people working in healthcare assumed that the arrangement of physicians, hospitals, technology, and insurance was all that was required to deliver high-quality care. Hospitals in most communities provide the tools for physicians to use. New pharmacological and electronic technology developments supported increased specialization believed by most people to be the basis for achieving high-quality healthcare. Insurance programs through the government or work provided most people with access to hospitals, and hospitals provided charity care to assist people without means or insurance.

The primary drivers of this new direction were the cost of healthcare to the federal government, which increased significantly after the implementation of Medicare and Medicaid in 1965, and the cost of healthcare insurance to employers who were fighting the economic war with a newly empowered Japan in the 1980s. It gained momentum in the 2000s as the Institute of Medicine published a series of reports on the status of healthcare errors, quality, and costs and what needed to be done to improve healthcare (IOM 1999, 2001, 2012). Data from a variety of sources indicated that the high costs of American healthcare relative to costs around the world were not producing high levels of quality. As data became more and more available through the Medicare program and research, it became clear that much of the costs of American healthcare resulted from variations in care, overutilization of services, and poor quality (IOM 2012; Dartmouth Health Atlas 2014). American healthcare's inability to address the cost and quality concerns beyond protests of uniqueness, bad data, and technological superiority fueled the sense that the answer to the dilemma lies outside of the traditional circles of healthcare. Industrialization infiltrated healthcare from industry due to healthcare's inability to respond to the problems that had become so apparent (Berwick et al. 1990).

The development of Henry Ford's assembly line in the early 1900s demonstrated the ability of American industry to produce massive quantities of goods very quickly (Hounshell 1984). These same processes could generate large quantities of defective as well as good products without a means for determining the quality of the products prior to reaching the end of the assembly lines. In the 1930s, Walter Shewhart developed control charts to measure variability in samples of product from a production line. With the control chart, employees on the assembly line could identify the variation and if it was great enough to warrant intervention in the process (Shewhart 1980).

American industry did not embrace Shewhart's work. During World War II, the ability to produce massive quantities of good-enough war materials took precedent over improving quality. As the victors, American industry had no reason to change their methods following the war. W. Edwards Deming worked with Shewhart and understood his ideas on quality. He presented them along with his own views on improving quality to the Japanese to help in their reconstruction effort after the war. Shewhart focused specifically on process improvement using statistical variation, but the industrial quality taught to the Japanese by Deming and Joseph Juran and refined by Armand Feigenbaum focused on the entire production process. This new approach included suppliers, customers, the engagement of management, and the entire organization in the production of high-quality goods and services. By expanding responsibility for quality to management, these quality leaders gave Japan the critical insight that led to their impressive performance 20 years later (Berwick et al. 1990; Dobyns and Crawford-Mason 1991). Japan used this new information, their own efforts exemplified in the Toyota Production System, and Ishikawa quality circles to create a new production method based on continuous improvement that engages the entire organization. By the 1980s, American industry found itself fighting an uphill battle against high-quality Japanese products, particularly in the automotive and electronics fields (Dobyns and Crawford-Mason 1991; Womack et al. 2007).

As American industrial leaders worked through their wounded pride and financial losses and actually began to study Japan's achievements, some of them recognized the value in what the Japanese had developed and the importance of organization-wide involvement in continuous quality improvement. Motorola, in particular, took the lessons to heart and began their own quality journey in the 1980s. Through the efforts of Bill Smith, Mikel Harry, and others, Motorola brought together the best of new quality thinking and added a special touch of their own. They decided to pursue nearly perfect products by setting their defect rate at 3.4-defects-per-million opportunities or a Six Sigma rate. To achieve this goal, they realized that they could no longer focus only on the production line. They also had to focus on reducing the defects in the processes leading up to the production line. Rather than simply producing products that are within the margin of error for their customers, Motorola continuously improved their processes to meet the exact specifications for their customers. In this way, the company created an improvement methodology that won them the Malcolm Baldrige National Quality Award during its first year (Harry and Schroeder 2000).

Just as American industry woke up to the realization that Japan had surpassed it in quality, 20th century American healthcare awoke in the first decade of the 21st century to face the growing evidence that its quality no longer met world standards. Even more importantly, the government, employers, and the public viewed the costs of American healthcare as unsustainable. Quality efforts within American healthcare throughout the 20th century involved primarily credentialing and licensing physicians and other practitioners and surveys and accreditation of hospitals by the American College of Surgeons and later the Joint Commission on Accreditation of Hospitals (JCAH). Attempts at improvement included the work of Avedis Donabedian (1980) in the 1960s that established the process, structure, and outcome model, the JCAH Organization's Agenda for Change in 1987 that redesigned accreditation, and the initiation of the ORYX program in 1997 that required accredited hospitals to submit standardized core measure performance data. After Medicare became a law in 1965, the Conditions of Participation in the Medicare program set minimal standards for hospitals along with accreditation surveys (Lohr 1990). These efforts surveyed only the basics required for hospital operations. The federal government implemented the Healthcare Maintenance Organization Act in 1973 to focus on reducing costs through preventative care and better management of care. Medicare implemented the prospective payment system in the 1980s to set reimbursement rates to reduce the rapidly increasing costs to the federal government. Despite the initial efforts, healthcare costs continued to rise for Medicare, and commercial insurers and 20th century American healthcare did not develop an effective response. This opened the door for solutions from outside of healthcare (IOM 2012).

The initial steps toward introducing industrialization in the form of industrial quality in American healthcare on a meaningful level to address problems of cost and quality may have begun with the work of Paul Batalden, MD, in the 1980s. After attending a seminar taught by Deming in 1981, he contributed to Deming's book, *Out of the Crisis*. After struggling to find a channel for applying Deming's work to healthcare, Batalden met with Thomas F. Frist, Jr., MD, the Chief Executive Officer (CEO) of Hospital Corporation of America (HCA), in 1986 and encouraged him to implement training on Deming's ideas at HCA. HCA at the time owned more than 400 hospitals. Frist agreed, and Batalden went to work at HCA in the Quality Resource Group until 1992, training thousands of HCA employees in Deming's concepts and methods for quality improvement and management. Batalden also introduced Don Berwick, MD, and Brent James, MD, to Deming. Berwick and Batalden continued to collaborate until 1991 when they developed the Institute for Healthcare Improvement (Kenney 2008).

In 1987, the National Demonstration Project brought together 21 healthcare organizations' quality experts to explore the question of whether the tools of modern quality improvement used in industry can be applied to healthcare. For the next eight months, the organizations worked to solve the question. In the end, improvements were made in areas of the healthcare organizations similar to those in industry such as billing, wait times, and discharge processes but no attempts at improvements in clinical processes (Berwick et al. 1990).

Despite the successes of industry and the work of Batalden, Berwick, and others, the concepts and techniques associated with the industrial quality movement did not flood into healthcare organizations. In fact, 20th century American healthcare demonstrated itself to be amazingly resistant to pressure to change. Signs of change, however, began to appear the first decade of the 21st century, and the industrialization phase of American healthcare has begun albeit slowly. A useful way to identify progress in industrialization in healthcare organizations is to look for signs of quality management and performance improvement. Some healthcare organizations, such as Virginia Mason Medical Center and ThedaCare, developed Lean methodologies in their organizations to the point that it has become part of their organizational brand. These programs began in the early 2000s to 2002 for Virginia Mason and 2003 for ThedaCare—and have become models for other organizations interested in learning from them (Kenney 2008).

Looking through the special lenses of industrialization, what does American healthcare look like with the application of industrial quality methods? In looking broadly at healthcare organizations today from the perspective of industrial quality improvement, it is clear that hospitals have been engaged in some type of quality improvement for years. Many federal, state, and accreditation agencies have had standards and requirements that healthcare organizations implement performance or quality improvement plans, structures, and initiatives at least since the 2000s. Surveying agencies look for specific indications of methods of improvement and signs of actual improvement within hospitals and other healthcare organizations. In looking from one organization to the next, however, there would be very little consistency in methods of improvements as each healthcare organization customizes their quality plans and projects to fit their culture and structure.

In addition to structures and processes designed by individual hospitals to meet standards, mandatory reporting of data has increased in the last decade as the Centers for Medicare and Medicaid Services (CMS) began to require clinical process data from hospitals and other healthcare providers. Using abstracted data from healthcare organizations and Medicare claims, CMS has begun to post comparative hospital, nursing home, and other data on various websites to aid consumers in selection care providers. CMS began reporting on Hospital Compare in 2005 with 10 clinical measures. It expands the information available on the website on a regular basis. The website offers a comparison of performance on these measures from one hospital to another with the goals of encouraging potential patients to evaluate their choices for care (Hospital Quality Initiative Overview 2008).

Initial evidence that healthcare organizations perceive industrial quality techniques as part of their quality improvement efforts comes from required data reporting by the CMS and the JCAH and evidence of quality training offered by healthcare agencies and professional associations that focus on data and specific improvement techniques. These elements of industrial quality began in the last decades of the 20th century but only in a limited sense. Their use signaled the initial efforts of agencies to bring industrialization into healthcare organizations (Kenney 2008).

As you view American healthcare through the lenses of industrialization and look for the distinguishing characteristics of industrial quality that differ from the past, your search begins with the customer. For Lean, Six Sigma, and other industrial quality methods, customers define the need for products or services and describe what is valuable and what they are willing to pay for (Ohno 1988). As you search for this person across American healthcare, you will find that there is no one who clearly fits this description. You hear the term "customer" used and see some indications of customers associated with processes of improvement but no indication of a customer who meets the concepts of industrial quality.

Looking for the customer of industrialization in healthcare, you focus your attention on the physician as a good candidate to serve as the customer. The physician orders the services; describes what is valuable; and specifies when, where, and how to deliver the services. The physician determines if the services met expectations. These represent activities of a customer. You realize, however, that the physician does not pay for the service, and the physician does not ultimately receive the service. Even as an intermediate recipient of information, the physician is only marginally in a position to engage as a customer. Since the information does not directly affect the physician, and the method of testing and other activities for obtaining the information do not directly affect the physician, the physician does not have a personal engagement as the customer. Finally, the physician does not pay for the information obtained through the process. Though there are elements in healthcare processes that point to the physician as the customer from the perspective of industrialization, the physician fails in a number of ways.

Using your industrial lenses, you look at the patient and wonder if this is the customer of industrialized healthcare. The patients receive the services provided by healthcare organizations as the end of the processes of care, and the delivery of the care directly affects them. The patients, however, are not the ones who describe the product or service, and no one asks them what is valuable to them about the service. The patients do not answer the questions that industrialization requires of the customer: What service do you need? Where would you like to receive it? When is it convenient for you? How would you like to receive it? What is valuable to you about this service? What are you willing to pay for this service?

You suddenly realize that there is no one who fulfills the role of the customer as defined by industrialization in 20th century healthcare organizations. Neither the physician nor the patient meets the requirements for the customer that is at the center of industrialization and industrial quality. Without a customer who fulfills the role in the delivery of healthcare services, the methods of industrialization result in only marginal changes. As you consider this, you realize that much of the cost and quality issues in healthcare result from the failure to identify an industrialized customer. The physician as the customer does not pay for the service. The design and delivery of the service do not directly affect the physician. Only the person receiving the service and directly affected by the cost can provide the parameters required by industry to deliver the service. The patient also fails as the customer because the healthcare organization does not design the services based on what the patient considers valuable or what he/she agrees to pay. The physician designs the service and identifies the value, and the insurance company pays for it. Industrialization begins with the customer and his/her requirements. Without this important participant in the creation, delivery, and pricing of a service, methods such as Lean and Six Sigma are only marginally effective.

Your next step in looking for signs of the industrialization of healthcare is to find the product. You search for the product that the customer purchases. The customer defines the product and determines its value. You realize that from the industrial perspective of the nature of a product, the patient comes closest to actually being the product. At this point, you recognize one of the dilemmas of 20th century healthcare as it moves toward industrialization. The patient could not fulfill the role of the customer in the industrial sense because the patient did not design the services or determine the value, and the patient did not pay for the services. You realize that the patient is the product of healthcare from an industrial perspective. The patient is the material changed by the processes of the healthcare organization. The professional staff retained all the control and information about the care processes, and the patient complied with the requirements for achieving those goals. Ultimately, the patient is the product improved or defective at the end of the healthcare production process (Goodwin 2015).

As you struggle to determine the customer and the product of healthcare, you finally realize that the patient is the customer as well as the product from the perspective of industrial quality. This realization opens the way for a new understanding of how healthcare organizations will operate as industrialization progresses. The recognition of the patient as patient/product and as patient/customer transfers the focus of the organization from the healthcare professionals who were the *de facto* customers of the past to the patients as customers and the product of their relationship with the organization.

The patient-customer's desires, expectations, and values become the basis for the development and design of services. The voice of the patient as the voice of the customer must be at the table whenever the organization makes improvements or initiates new services. Industrialization requires continuous information flow between the organization and the patient-customer to refine services and respond to changes in expectations.

Simultaneously, the patient as the product continues to be an individual changed by the processes of the organization. The organization progressing into industrialization must recognize that the patient as the customer will evaluate the care process and the results of the care. During the actual care process, the healthcare professionals taking care of the patient often make decisions based on clinical judgment and without consulting the patient in order to meet the agreed-upon goals of the patient. This is appropriate given the role of the professional in the actual production of the services. The evaluation and outcomes of care, however, bring the patient as the customer forward to assess the quality of the care.

One question that comes to your mind as you consider the patient-customer is the issue of payment. The patient as the customer receives the services, and the services delivered by the organization change the patient as the product; the patient often does not pay for the services and, therefore, does not meet that requirement of the customer from the industrial quality perspective. There are two ways to approach this aspect of the patient-customer. The first is to recognize that the patient-customers receive the services and actually have the services performed on them. From this perspective, the patients legitimately function as customers in evaluating the services delivered to them. The second is that businesses and the government are shifting more of the payment for healthcare to the patient-customers through high-deductible insurance plans. Insurance companies require patients to assume first dollar responsibility and very significant overall payment responsibility in the thousands of dollars prior to the insurers making any payments. As patients assume more of this new responsibility, their role as patient-customers becomes much clearer. Recognizing this new patient-customer status is an indication that healthcare organizations have begun to implement industrialization.

Value as defined by the customer is an integral part of industrial quality, and it is a critical aspect for the industrialization phase of healthcare. In the development of services and redesign of processes, the voice of the patient-customer must guide healthcare organizations in creating and delivering services that they consider valuable and worth the payment. Patient-customers determining value transforms organizations because of the difference from 20th century healthcare organizations. As you shift your gaze to the 20th century lenses and look for the expressions of the concepts of value, you find the physicians and other clinical staff making that determination but not the patient as the customer. The patient of the 20th century did not define the value of a service and would consider the request to identify the value of services as inappropriate in the same way that the physicians and clinical staff would have seen their participation as unusual.

The role of patient-customers in the industrial sense is so new that most patients would simply prefer that the professionals decide what is valuable. The problem with this is that it distorts the concept of value by shifting it into a professional environment rather than into the world of the patient-customer. In the professional environment, the personal preferences of the professionals become the determining factors in the design and delivery of services and the goals expected from the services. Since the professionals neither receive the services nor pay for them, their preferences are secondary. In this new world of industrialized quality, it is not enough for healthcare to satisfy the professionals who deliver the services. The services must provide recognizable value to the patient-customers. The healthcare organizations must find ways to learn what is valuable from their patient-customers through whatever means they can devise.

The importance of identifying value in healthcare is more than just meeting the expectations and desires of patient-customers. Waste is what patient-customers do not consider valuable. The elimination of waste is the basis for reducing the costs of healthcare. Industrialization requires healthcare organizations to identify and eliminate services that patient-customers do not consider valuable. One of the significant lessons that Taiichi Ohno taught the world through his work at Toyota was the importance of identifying and eliminating waste wherever it occurs. He identified seven types of waste and was obsessive about their elimination. His efforts at eliminating waste at Toyota enabled the company to increase its margin per automobile sold without sacrificing quality because eliminating waste reduced costs. The basis for identifying waste is anything that does not add value as determined by the customer or anything that the customer is not willing to pay for or purchase (Ohno 1988).

Looking through the industrialization lenses of your glasses provides you with the means to see into healthcare processes and to consider what patient-customers would consider valuable and what they would consider waste. The first step is to determine what the patient-customers will pay for a service or process by asking them what they consider valuable and worth the payment. The next step is to evaluate each aspect of the service or process to assess whether it meets the criteria of value established by the patient-customers. If it does not, the organization should eliminate it if possible. Since waiting and delays in processes are waste, waiting rooms in many organizations would be considered wasteful and need to be eliminated. Industrialization of healthcare produces this level of transformation.

Waiting and delays are waste, and flow is an indicator of the presence or absence of waste in a process or a service. If the process flows smoothly, delays or waiting does not compromise the service for the patient-customers. Continuous flow with the regular processing of patient-customers rather than making patients wait and sending them through in a group or batch provides more value and less waste. As you observe healthcare organizational processes and services through your industrialization lenses, you easily recognize the flow of support services such as laundry, food service, and room cleaning services. Staff arranges signals to alert these services to respond. The organization monitors the responses and the completion of the services to evaluate waste resulting from delays. You can easily detect delays or waiting that indicates problems with the flow of the processes. Hospital administrations have long focused on timely delivery of support services because they are easy to monitor and play an important role in the overall efficiency of the hospital.

Applying the concept of flow to patient-customers, however, is where industrialization of healthcare brings a new dimension to the concept. There are aspects of patient care that clearly evidence movement such as transfers from the emergency department to the inpatient units. For many patient-customers who remain in specific rooms throughout their hospital care, the concept of flow resembles that of people dining at a restaurant. People dining at a restaurant do not flow or move from the table during the meal. The patient-customers remain in the room, and there is no visible evidence of flow during the time they are in the hospital. It is in these cases that the concept of flow becomes especially important because the progress of the patient toward discharge comes from changes in the patient-customer, but it is invisible to the people around the patient. With no way to know visible cues of the patient's progress toward discharge, delays, and interruptions are difficult to see and improve.

Since the patient does not move, the focus is on the flow of the services that serve the patient and the outcome in terms of the length of time before the patient can leave. Through your industrialization lenses, however, you recognize that the patient is at the center of an array of processes and services designed to resolve the health issue and to discharge the patient. These interconnected processes all must function well to achieve the optimum outcome for the patient.

Through your lenses, you see a flowchart image of the many processes and all of the ways that they can fail. Standardization is the basis for sustaining the best practices in the various processes and ultimately achieving the best outcomes. Standardization to best practice with continuous improvement was a key part of Toyota and Six Sigma's success (Ohno 1988; Harry and Schroeder 2000). As you let your view move to the 20th century lenses, you see that professional judgment and personal preferences of professional staff played an important role in the design of process in 20th century healthcare organizations. Since physicians often practiced in their offices and in the hospital, hospital processes accommodated the schedules of practitioners, and delays were common. Disagreements between practitioners led to different processes depending on who was taking care of the patient, and the support staff had to accommodate these differences even though the preference of the physicians rather than the condition of the patient produced them. At the same time, the policies and procedures of the hospital or healthcare organization described what the hospital staff should do; the physicians often view these policies as guidelines that they can disregard.

Standardization is a critically important part of the industrialization process because it requires that everyone recognize the best practice for a process and follow that best practice unless the patient's condition requires a change. This means that the professional staff recognizes the value of standardization and honors the design of the process unless there is a valid reason for negotiating a change. Shewhart and Deming preached the basic concept that you cannot improve an unstable process, and deviation from the steps in the process is the principle reason for the instability of a standardized process (Shewhart 1980; Dobyns and Crawford-Mason 1991). The work of gaining acceptance, particularly from the professional staff, for the importance of following standardized processes is an important cultural aspect of the industrialization of healthcare.

Motorola's commitment to the pursuit of nearly perfect production processes focused on the specifications provided by the customers. For each product, customers provided a range for variation that they considered acceptable. As long as the part or process was within the specifications, they consider it acceptable. Part of the success of Motorola in achieving Six Sigma quality was due to the recognition that they needed to achieve perfect performance in all of the operations of a process or service rather than simply addressing defects that occur on the assembly line. This meant that each operation feeding into process must be as close as possible to the customer's specifications if the entire process is going to achieve a Six Sigma rate of defects (Harry and Schroeder 2000). Standardization, closely monitoring variation, and continuous improvement are required to ensure that organizations meet the specifications. Healthcare organizations in the 20th century did not even consider the possibility of this level of performance. Customers expect manufacturing and service industries to deliver nearly perfect service. Patient-customers expect healthcare organizations to match that performance, and this expectation opened the way for the industrialization of healthcare.

If achieving Six Sigma levels of performance requires statistical analysis of variation, it is clear that healthcare must develop a new appreciation for the importance of data in improvement and the standardization of process. Data collection and analysis at the point of care and in all aspects of the organization distinguish the industrialization of healthcare from the professionally defined levels of quality produced in 20th century organizations. Monitoring processes and performance improvement rarely occurred in healthcare institutions in the 20th century due to the lack of real-time performance data and the lack of training of staff in the use of data in daily operations.

For healthcare organizations, the monitoring of operational data to maintain high levels of performance and to identify deviation in standardized processes represents an important challenge as part of industrialization. It requires that equipment in the operational areas capture and display important information on the degree to which the care delivered on the unit meets the goals of the organization. It also means training the staff to understand data and to be able to respond to it. When the specifications of patient-customers set the goals for operations, high performance is an expectation of all healthcare organizations. Healthcare organizations must be able to recognize breakdowns in processes and delays in services as quickly as possible and address them quickly to limit the impact on patient-customers.

The importance of rapid response to changes in operations that affect patient-customers brings into view the role of management in industrial quality and the industrialization of healthcare organizations. The active engagement of management in responding to breakdowns that threatened the quality or the flow of product made the difference in the success of Japanese manufacturing in achieving high levels of quality with minimal waste. The ability of anyone to stop the production line in order to prevent the spread of defects was part of the success, but the immediate response of the leadership to assess the issue and support changes reduced the impact of problems.

In 20th century healthcare, the lack of an understanding of the interconnectedness of all elements of the organization and the tendency to focus on individuals rather than systems in identifying problems made it difficult to find and fix problems in the system. As the industrialization phase brings a new perspective to American healthcare, the emphasis will shift from the individual to the processes and from the lone staff person patching together a quick fix to management rapidly bringing resources to the area to support a remedy. Too often in the past, the warrior spirit of healthcare celebrated the ability of staff to get through the day or night working around problems to provide care to patients but without fixing the problems. Industrialization celebrates standardization that provides the staff with the best processes possible. It rewards the ability of staff to identify waste in the form of defects and delays and to recommend improvements. Finally, leadership supports the work of staff in improving processes by responding quickly whenever problems occur and providing resources to assist staff.

Looking through the lenses of industrialization opens a new perspective on the way that healthcare operates. As 20th century American healthcare enters the industrialization phase specifically to remedy the cost and quality issues, the application of industrial quality to 20th century organizations results in significant changes that overwhelm the structures, values, and practices of the past and opens the organizations to a new way of operating. For healthcare organizations to achieve the quality and cost goals required in the 21st century, fully implementing industrialization and opening their operations to the voice of patient-customers bring forth the transitions that lead to the future.

Chapter 5

21st Century American Healthcare

Beyond the industrialization phase of American healthcare, the 21st century opens up as a new perspective for healthcare that incorporates the remaining elements of the 20th century, the dynamics of industrialized healthcare, and the many new aspects of healthcare that appear as new technology and new delivery methods appear. Organizational, process, and cultural changes shape healthcare organizations in the 21st century as they adapt to the new environment in which patient-customers assume a dominant and more active role in the design, delivery, and evaluation of services. Significant new dynamics in the healthcare landscape shift more of the costs of healthcare to the patient, and new technology transformations open new options for delivering care. As patients struggle to manage the costs of care, they constantly challenge the healthcare delivery system to offer better services at less cost. New technological developments challenge 21st century healthcare by offering patient-customers the ability to obtain care through different delivery processes for less than the traditional methods.

In addition to the cost and technology drivers of the healthcare delivery system, the subtle change from acute care organizations such as hospitals as the primary source of healthcare to an emphasis on preventative care begins to have an effect on the need for services. As patient-customers assume more costs, they look for ways to avoid using healthcare services. They turn to new sources of information that offer ways to improve their health and reduce the need of healthcare services. They use their new buying power to purchase services that are less expensive and more convenient, and they take a more active role in defining their own goals for care.

As you shift your gaze to the 21st century lenses of your glasses, you are somewhat surprised to see the difference in the landscape of healthcare compared to the 20th century and the industrial phase. The implications of the changes you saw occurring in industrialization appear now as you view 21st century healthcare organizations, and their effect exceeds your expectations.

You begin to assess what appear to be dramatically different ways organizations, patient-customers, and healthcare professionals interact, and you realize that 21st century healthcare is truly different from what came before it.

Looking at the healthcare organizations themselves, you find a new relationship between the employees of the organization and the patient-customers. Where the staff and the patient-customers interact, the conversations and perspectives have changed. Employees serving the patient-customers ask more questions about the preferences, desires, and expectations of people coming for service. Employees offer more choices and more information and encourage the patient-customers to express their concerns about their care and to describe what they feel would best serve them.

Most interesting in these interactions is the extensive information systems that are used by the employees and the patient-customers. As they talk, the employees and the patient-customers are reviewing information, and the employee is entering the comments and directions of the patient-customers. Together, they create a description of what is to happen with the patient-customer and what the desires and expectations of the person receiving the services are. Whenever the patient-customer raises issues that require more information, the employee enters that request into the computer to alert other employees in the system to obtain the answer before the patient-customer leaves. Employees address questions or concerns addressed quickly or research answers.

The employee listens as patient-customers call and express their concerns about the care they received. The employee enters the information in the system. As the patient-customer concludes their comments, the employee quickly reviews the issues, identifies the expectations, and reduces the patient-customer's bill. A message sent to the care area involved describes the concerns with the customer's ideas for improvement. The business office will send a check to the customer in appreciation for calling. Behind the scenes, exchanges between employees in various areas relay information from the interactions with patient-customers. They use the information systems to quickly review any problems or concerns in real time and provide information to the employee directly involved with the patient-customers.

All of the employees involved in working with patients directly and behind the scenes have the ability to communicate with anyone who may be able to help provide information or participate in the resolution. As they work to resolve any issues, they all know the four simple rules that the organization has established to operationalize the mission, vision, and values and to guide the interaction with patient-customers. These rules emphasize respect and courtesy, work together to solve the problem for the patient-customer, identify any ideas or innovative improvements that arise from the interactions, and assess the success in satisfying the patient-customer.

You are impressed as the communications and interactions from employees in various areas converge to work out issues and then shift to new areas to address other issues. The complexity of the interactions, the flow of communications, and the way the system continuously adapts as new issues arise come from the interactions of the people involved. You search for the hierarchy or central structure, but it is hard to see in the myriad of conversations and interactions shaping the relationships between employees and patient-customers. It appears that the organization forms as a system out of the complexity of the repeated interactions of everyone involved in delivering and receiving the services.

As employees in the 21st century healthcare organization work together and with the patient-customers, you are impressed with the breadth of their activities and the way in which they move from one activity to another. They spend most of their time engaged with the information system and following the directions set out in that system for their activities. Employees find most of their routine activities described and prompted in the systems with guides for policies and procedures.

New employees appear to spend most of their first days in the organization focusing on the mission, vision, values, and four operational rules. During the orientation time, they are engaged in discussion with the current staff in talking about the ways in which the organization expresses its fundamental principles in the life of the employees and their interactions with each other and with patient-customers. The importance of operationalizing the mission, vision, and values in the four rules takes up most of the time. Current employees emphasize the depth of the resources in the information system and the importance of each employee in recognizing their ability to respond to issues within the scope of the four rules. They point out that the specific individual job responsibilities are guided by the information system and the importance of responding to the prompts and guides in the system to complete the work. They emphasize, however, that employees create their jobs as they work together to solve problems, identify innovative ways to improve services, and satisfy patient-customers. Their evaluations and incentives arise out of these activities.

The role of leadership within the context of the complex system is more difficult to see. The 20th century and the industrial-phase healthcare organizations operated with clearly delineated positions of power at the top and middle levels of the organizations that emphasized control and upward reporting of results of work. In the 21st century, leadership has become a system function rather than a position. Individuals who hold positions of power express leadership within the organization by modeling the mission, vision, and values and offering support to employees. Rather than cloistered in suites of offices, they are talking with the employees who have the most contact with patient-customers in clinical and non-clinical areas. They are constantly monitoring the information system for activities related to patient-customer concerns or complaints. They praise employees who perform well and encourage them to take the initiative in organizing responses to problems and in trying innovative ideas. All the time, leadership offers support for the efforts and models the use of the four rules.

Using various methods of communication, leaders who also hold positional power talk about recent patient-customer issues that were resolved and issues

36 ■ *Mapping the Path to 21st Century Healthcare*

addressed by employees. They share with everyone the state of the organization and the areas of success and concern on a frequent basis and provide current data on key metrics related to operations and patient-customer responses. They share examples of innovations initiated by staff throughout the organization and encourage everyone to listen to the patient-customers for more ideas for improvement. The leadership emphasizes trust and support for employees rather than control. Adherence to the four rules and the mission, values, and vision form the key accountabilities for the employees and the leaders.

As you watch interactions between clinical and nonclinical employees with patient-customers, you notice how frequently employees are taking notes on the comments and suggestions made by patient-customers. Employees share these notes with coworkers and innovation groups on a regular basis. Employees request resources and time to develop innovations resulting from interactions with patient-customers. On their daily rounds, employees ask about new ideas and recent innovations and what is needed to move them forward. Awards are offered frequently to staff who develop new ways to improve patient-customer satisfaction, reduce waste, and come up with new ideas for services.

You recognize as you watch these activities shift from the centralized innovation of the 20th century healthcare organizations and move to innovation based on interactions with patient-customers. The innovations that employees identify through their interactions provide the opportunity for the organization to adapt to the changing needs and expectations of patient-customers. The innovations are the new requests for services or complaints about existing services that alert the organization on ways to adapt. Employees use their implicit knowledge of the work and their knowledge of the organization to develop innovative responses to the comments from patient-customers.

Wherever you look in the 21st century healthcare organization, you see groups of all sizes working together. In clinical areas, you see what look like physicians in groups with other healthcare professionals, but it is not clear because there is no distinguishing clothing. It is clear, however, that the group is working together and not subordinates waiting on the directions from a specific individual as was so common with physicians in the 20th century healthcare organizations. All of the members of the groups are active and participating in the issue. The familiarity of the group and the way it is working through problems indicate that this is a common occurrence and not a special meeting. This is not an environment that supports an individual expert craftsman but rather a care process that is born out of the dynamic interaction of all of the members of the group. As the group discusses the care of the patients, each person adds their voice and a perspective that contributes to the discussion and enriches the group.

Looking closer at the groups through the 21st century lenses, you recognize on the name badges designations for a variety of disciplines that are clinical and nonclinical. The discussions range from specifically clinical issues to financial and social issues. Looking closer, you realize that in the midst of the group are the patient and the family members. At first, you did not notice them because they are as active as the other clinicians and participants in the discussion. As you watch, the patient is holding a computer tablet and pointing to the screen while asking questions. Individuals in the group are taking notes, and others are responding to the questions from the patient or the family members. The patient seems comfortable in the discussion and not reticent to ask additional questions in response to the answers. The comfort of the patient as a participant in the discussion is far different from the patients in the 20th century who simply accepted directions from the physicians (Lindberg et al. 2008).

Though you initially focused your attention on the hospital as a convenient starting point, you now look out toward the community through your 21st century lenses, and you are suddenly amazed to see connections flowing out of the hospital to a variety of care providers in the community. As you follow these connections, you realize that the hospital is actually one part of a continuum of care and not even the central part of the way it was in the 20th century healthcare delivery system. As you look around, you are not seeing a center. Each home seems to be connected, and looking closer at the homes, you realize that the computer in the home is the origin of the connection to the continuum of care. Individuals receive care through televisits over their computer. They join discussion groups for specific diseases and look up the latest information on their condition from websites. They check their medical records through the portals to their primary care office. They store workout data on their computers as well as weight, heart rate, hours of sleep, calorie counts, blood sugar, and a variety of values related to their health that are fed into the computer from devices in their homes. The computer in their home has become the center of their continuum of care.

Following the connections from the home out into the community, the diversity is astounding. Cost and convenience are important aspects of care based on the number of flows that you see to wellness centers, pharmacies, retail clinics, chiropractors, urgent care, imaging centers, laboratory facilities, ambulatory surgery centers, and multispecialty office practices. Tablets and smartphones provide access to schedules for patient-customers to make their own appointments to fit their schedules. Easy and secure access to health information based on the authorization by the patient-customers comes through a centralized health information exchange. You find that the 21st century continuum of care offers more services and more convenience to facilitate care that works for patient-customers. Through their choices, they are able to manage their care and reduce their costs.

In following the connections in the continuum of care through your 21st century lenses, you are particularly impressed with the way in which computer systems integrate into a broad network that makes information readily available to providers and to patient-customers and reduces the isolation that created the potential for errors in care in the 20th century. You remember the 20th century healthcare organizations in which isolated computers in individual departments with stand-alone programs did not integrate with any systems. Hospital and office personnel combined paper copies of computer reports into the medical records of patients.

In the 21st century, however, you see a centralized health information exchange that is open to all the providers authorized to access patient information. A secure network provides the link for various care providers that is also open to the patient-customers through their portal. Care delivered at each site contributes information on the patient-customers that the healthcare exchange stores in a cloud that accommodates access by all of the individual systems. Patient-customers and providers are able to access this information in real time.

With all the various choices for care, you wonder how the patient-customers work out the financial arrangements. You remember the 20th century fee-for-services that took care of the payments, but the insurance only covered the physician and the hospital. As you adjust your 21st century lenses, you see the continuum of care spread out before you with a broad spectrum of services and providers. Looking in on the patient-customers as they arrange care at their computers or on their tablets, you realize that healthcare financing works like other financial accounts. For many patient-customers, they are the first payers for their care for employer-sponsored commercial health insurance. For Medicare and other programs, patients also have deductibles. They review their health savings accounts and the portion of their deductible that remains before the insurance company provides coinsurance or full coverage. This all seems so much more complicated than the system in the past, but then you also realize that the information on the screen looks like an investment account or bank account, and the patient-customers seem to be able to understand their healthcare financing.

As patient-customers move from their health insurance and health savings account, you are amazed at the number of other sites paid through their health savings account. Their fitness club membership and their fresh vegetable co-op membership dues all come out of their health savings account. You observe them searching for a local imaging center for a scan. They review the bundled prices for each procedure and find their scan and all its elements including the scan, contrasts, supplies, interpretation, and other expenses in one price. Each procedure lists overall quality ratings and a number of complications for specific procedures for the past three years. After reviewing several imaging centers and their patient-customer ratings on online healthcare rating sites, the patient-customers choose the lowest-cost, highest-quality center and e-mail their physician office their choice. Patient-customers have access to a wide variety of services. Most of the services offer transparency and bundled pricing along with standardized quality ratings and complication rates as normal business practices for the industry.

As patients access care, they have a variety of financing options to help them manage costs. Beginning with health savings accounts, patient-customers pay for their services until their insurance coverage begins. When the cost of care exceeds their savings, and they have not fulfilled their deductible, patient-customers arrange financing with the providers of services who often offer financial terms to attract new business. Patient-customers also make arrangements through their banks or credit cards to cover care costs. With access to cost and quality information for most of the services and providers, patient-customers are able to look for value in their healthcare purchasers.

As you think about all that you have seen of 21st century healthcare organizations and systems, you realize that one of the most profound changes has been the change from the professional autonomy of 20th century healthcare to the integration of the physicians into the overall delivery of care. Throughout the continuum of care, physicians are actively involved in all of the services and provide leadership, guidance, and direction to other healthcare disciplines in the design and delivery of healthcare. The difference in the 21st century is that the physician no longer makes decisions alone as the only voice determining the care of the patient-customers. The complexity of the healthcare system and the rapid changes in technology and care processes require a multidisciplinary team care for the patient-customers' conditions and to manage the many options in terms of care, convenience, and costs to meet their needs.

The professional autonomy of the past designed to protect the pricing power and status of the physician no longer operates within a system in which pricing is transparent, and services are competitively priced and delivered by professionals at all levels. With primary care televisits at less than $50, walk-in retail outlets, and competitive pricing in imaging and laboratories, there is no way for physicians to compete by hiding behind the professional autonomy of the 20th century.

Even within the hospital setting, the quality and cost standards that must be met preclude the physicians from claiming sole responsibility for the care of patients. Information systems, standardized orders, protocols, and multidisciplinary teams monitor the status of patient-customers. Decision-support software offers guidance and tracks the orders continuously. Systems monitor the patient and implement protocols for care as they are needed with prompts to the professional care staff. In this environment, mistakes are costly to the organization and to the patient-customers, and the pursuit of perfection in the delivery of care requires a number of specialties managing the care.

As you try to bring together all the things that you have seen in 20th century healthcare, the industrialization phase, and 21st century healthcare, you search for some way to understand or create a picture of what these phases are all about and how to think about them. For the 20th century, the key image you find is science as the healthcare organizations grew in response to new technology and the professionalization of medicine. The bureaucracy of the hospital as it sought to control and manage all the activities described in the organizational chart reminds you of a machine. The machine image really took over during the industrialization phase of American healthcare. Industrialization incorporated the clinical aspects of care that were not brought under bureaucratic control in the 20th century healthcare organization into Lean and Six Sigma and the methods of industrial quality.

As you look through the lenses of the 21st century, you see the scientific machine image fade into the background as the complexity of the networks of computer information systems overwhelms any sense of control. In this environment, you begin to see healthcare as an enormous complex adaptive system that is constantly evolving and changing in response to its own internal dynamics as well as influences from the outside. The complexity comes from the myriad of people and groups and organizations linked through the information networks. As they interact, they adapt to each other and respond to the changing needs and expectations of their patient-customers. Within the thousands of interactions involved with the continuum of care, the system of care appears as employees shape their actions and decisions based on the mission, vision, and values that govern the operations of their organizations. The creative interactions of the people who deliver the care and the people who receive the care create this complex adaptive system that is 21st century healthcare every day.

As you shift your eyes from the 20th century lenses to the lenses of industrialization and finally to the 21st century, you think about the differences between the metaphors of the scientific machine of the 20th century, the industrial phase of American healthcare, and the emerging complex adaptive system of the 21st century. You are amazed at the evolution of American healthcare through these three phases. You see the flow as American healthcare grew up from village healers with limited training to new professionals with university educations to the hospitals with an ever-expanding array of technology. The hospital filled with technology and specialists represented the pinnacle of science and the confidence of modern society in fighting disease and even death. By its very existence, it produced the highest-quality care that humanity had ever imagined. The growing sophistication and cost of healthcare brought forth an equally sophisticated insurance industry that opened the doors to the wonders of hospital healthcare to millions of working people and later the elderly. As this scientific machine grew larger and larger, it required more resources until finally the cost of the great structure of healthcare threatened to overwhelm the society that created it. You imagine healthcare reaching out to industry for a lifeline. Industry threw Lean and Six Sigma life preservers into the swirling waters of cost threatening to drown American healthcare.

Industrialization brought more than healthcare expected as the pursuit of cost savings and higher quality challenged the structure, practices, and values of 20th century healthcare. Pulling in the clinical areas of healthcare that had escaped mechanization in the past, the efficient machine of healthcare industrialization used waste elimination, standardization, and data-driven perfection to purge the illusions of unique professionalism. In its place, the expectations and desires of the new patient-customers became the drivers of healthcare, and they demanded a system capable of constantly changing and improving to create the best care at lower costs with more choices and great convenience. The quaint hospital on the hill is now a dynamic complex adaptive system that responds not to the preferences of the professionals but rather to the expectations of the new patient-customers who demand better quality at lower cost as they make their decisions and pay the costs of healthcare.

PREPARING TO TRANSITION TO 21ST CENTURY HEALTHCARE

Chapter 6

Industrialization: Preparing to Transition

Healthcare organizations initiate industrialization and begin the process of addressing the issues of quality and costs by using industrial quality methods. It is important that healthcare organizations recognize that industrialization is not the destination but a phase of American healthcare development. Depending on how far the organizations go with industrialization, it may ultimately lead them to the ten transitions and the paths to 21st century healthcare. Knowing the challenges that lie ahead helps to reduce the sense of disorientation that comes from going in a particular direction but suddenly finding that the results of that decision seem to be taking you in another direction that you did not anticipate.

The initial challenge that faces healthcare organizations is to recognize that the implementation of industrialization in whatever form it takes is actually the first step in the move away from 20th century healthcare and toward the ten transitions to 21st century healthcare. This change comes from the pressures on organizations from a variety of sources, and the goal is to improve the processes of care in terms of costs and quality, but the result is that 20th century healthcare will no longer be American healthcare. Even the modest implementation of industrialization affects the older healthcare model and causes it to change but may not result in recognition of the ten transitions. American healthcare reaching full industrialization will be very different from the past, and the environment within which it functions and operates will be very different (Goodwin 2015).

Healthcare organizations that begin down the path of industrialization often progress only a short distance because the challenges from existing values, structures, and practices prevent them from reaching a higher degree of implementation. In order for transitions to appear and for the organizations to develop the vision necessary to move toward the 21st century, the organization must fully implement industrialization in all areas. It is only as the full implementation takes place that the conflict with the existing 20th century healthcare becomes clear, and the transitions appear. Industrialization that is only marginally implemented

43

changes the organization and produces a hybrid state similar to what many organizations are experiencing today, where industrialization exists as an attachment to 20th century healthcare, and the result is very confusing and relatively ineffective. Realizing the benefits of industrialization that are necessary for the transition to 21st century healthcare requires healthcare leaders to promote the implementation of industrial quality and industrialization into all aspects of their organizations (Goodwin 2015).

With the introduction of industrial quality and the spread of industrialization, healthcare organizations may become so engaged in industrialization that they view it as the endpoint. It is important that organizations recognize industrialization as a phase in the transformation of healthcare organizations. With industrialization, organizations are able to recognize and begin movement along ten transitions that represent the progression from 20th century healthcare to the new 21st century model. Leaders need to be knowledgeable about the nature of these transitions and to observe and map the overall transformation of their organizations by assessing their progress in the ten transitions. Tracking the movement through the ten transitions serves as the basis for assessing the overall transformation of their organization and their readiness to meet the demands of the future. By developing strategies to accelerate movement along the continuums within the ten transitions, leaders facilitate the movement of their organizations toward 21st century healthcare (Goodwin 2015).

Healthcare organizations need to understand that the power to realize the future is in the emerging images and concepts of 21st century healthcare that appear as industrialization advances. These images serve as guides and motivators to facilitate organizational transformation. Successfully moving into the future requires a clear vision of where the organization is going in each of the transitions. The images that emerge out of each of the transitions inspire and motivate employees and guide the changes. The images of the future within each transition guide the organization beyond industrialization. In order to continue the progress along the continuums of the transitions, however, the organizations must recognize the images of 21st century healthcare that appear in the transitions and actively use these visions of the future to motivate and guide their organizations (Goodwin 2015).

As the drumbeat of quality and costs pounded in the ears of 20th century American healthcare, the initial response was to declare that healthcare operated differently from any other aspect of society and that human life and human suffering required whatever resources were needed to reduce human suffering and save lives. This had been the protest against any form of national health insurance or regulation of healthcare and physicians throughout the 20th century. With the arrival of computers and particularly the Medicare claims database, and growing concerns about complications, injuries, death, as well as costs compared to other countries, the uniqueness of the position weakened, and the argument to apply industrial quality measures to American healthcare began to look like the answer. If American industry could absorb the new Japanese methods for eliminating waste, which actually began in America, and task itself with the goal of Six Sigma levels of quality, then American healthcare could at least learn the methods and try this approach (Berwick et al. 1990; IOM 2012).

This seemed like a reasonable argument to many policymakers and planners and others concerned with healthcare quality and costs, but it took decades from the initial suggestion until healthcare actually began in earnest to apply the concepts and techniques of industrial quality. The reason for the delay was also the reason for the problems that healthcare faced in changing its operations to improve quality and reduce costs. Healthcare operated on a split system of bureaucracy and professionalism that made it extremely difficult to mandate change, particularly in areas of clinical practice and patient care that generated the most costs and the quality issues.

When American healthcare moved the site of care for paying patients from the patient's home to the hospital in the early 20th century, the structure of the hospital changed. When physicians persuaded hospitals to purchase and staff new operating rooms, x-rays, and laboratories, there was a mutual agreement that the physician would bring their paying patients to the hospital, and the patients would pay for the hospital services as well as the physician services. This would help to defray the cost of the new technology and give the physicians access to the expensive new equipment. This increased not only the revenue stream to the hospital but also the organizational influence of the physicians as the source of paying patients. The new technology and the new patients also required a more sophisticated bureaucracy to manage the services.

As physicians migrated to the hospital in the early 20th century with their paying patients, they became more interested in hospital operations. Physicians organized into hospital medical staff to manage the clinical aspects of care in the hospital and to give them a stronger voice in requesting support from the hospital governing board of benefactors. The American College of Surgeons (2006) in their 1919 minimum standards set as the first three requirements specific provisions related to the medical staff, including "rules, regulations and policies governing professional work of the hospital..."

The medical staff as a professional affiliation within the hospital became a parallel organization to the hospital administration. The physicians through the medical staff operated on democratic principles of voting on members and on the rules and policies pertaining to the medical staff. Though the governing board approved the decisions of the medical staff, the board as nonphysicians was reluctant to upset physicians who were instrumental in bringing paying patients to the hospital. In reality, therefore, clinical practices that are the source of most of the costs and quality in hospitals fell within the purview of the medical staff rather than the administration throughout most of the 20th century.

With clinical care under the purview of the hospital medical staff, protests over cost and quality to hospital management resulted in few changes. The physicians as craftsman and professionals viewed any discussions about the cost and quality of clinical care as a strictly medical staff issue to be discussed within the confines of the professional affiliation of the medical staff. The best example for the limitations hospitals perceived to the introduction of industrial principles into healthcare was the 1987 National Demonstration Project. Not a single hospital that participated in the evaluation of applying industrial quality to healthcare undertook the improvement of clinical processes as part of the project. They worked on the less-sensitive hospital support services (Berwick et al. 1990). This highlights the division between what the nonphysician administration of healthcare controls and the areas that the medical staff controls. By limiting efforts to reduce costs and to improve quality only to the areas outside the control of the medical staff essentially meant that all clinical services were off limits to any changes that the medical staff felt were unacceptable. Using this divide enabled the medical staff in most hospitals to resist the intrusion of industrial practices and quality until the second decade of the 21st century.

The current pressure to improve the quality and cost of care for hospitals comes from two sources. The principal source is Medicare. Medicare penalizes hospitals financially for excessive complications, mortalities, injuries, readmissions, and costs as part of the agency's value-based purchasing and hospital-acquired condition programs. The financial penalties are not only substantial; they also are public. The publicity aspect grew out of the public displays of quality data that began in the 1990s with the Joint Commission on Accreditation of Hospitals' ORYX core measures and migrated to the Centers for Medicare and Medicaid Services (CMS) Hospital Compare website. As for the secondary source, commercial payers as well as CMS now use hospital data to reduce payments whenever the care of individual patients or overall care at the hospital fails to meet standards. Through these programs, data on quality of care affect hospital reimbursement.

Tying hospital reimbursement to clinical quality and outcomes does not directly affect the medical staff. Individual physicians and physician groups continue to be essentially unaffected financially or in terms of public display of quality data. As the penalties increase, however, hospitals feel the growing pressure to change. CMS has added the Physician Compare website, but there are very little data available. The medical staff retains its prerogatives related to clinical practices and rules and regulations governing practice in the hospital. These factors contribute to the difficulties hospitals experience in applying industrialization, Lean, and Six Sigma into clinical areas. Individual physicians and the medical staff resist the changes in clinical areas because the case for change is often not clear, and physician workflows and practice patterns are integral to their routines in the hospital and in their offices. As the frequency and severity of penalties increase, however, this may change, but it will take more time.

The transition of hospitals and other healthcare organizations to the industrialization phase will occur as the need to improve quality and costs reaches the crisis point. At that point, the medical staff and the hospital leadership structure may have a sufficiently strong common interest in improving quality and reducing costs to make it worthwhile to move forward. To achieve this next step, the medical staff will need to agree to the application of industrial quality to their practices and workflows in order for the organization to achieve the necessary improvements.

Industrialization to reduce costs and improve quality in healthcare organizations seems like any other program. For many senior managers, industrial quality looks like one more way to count but not a really new way of working. This approach views industrial quality as giving healthcare the ability to look good to society and then move on as a new lean healthcare machine. Often overlooked in the decision to adopt Lean and Six Sigma, however, is just how different they are from the essential nature of American healthcare. One measure of the unique nature of industrial quality as developed in Japan is the difficulty that American manufacturing had in deciphering the secrets of the Toyota Production System and Six Sigma even though they were developed by manufacturing companies and Americans.

The hard part about Lean and Six Sigma for American manufacturing was not the use of control charts to understand variation or the shift from mass production to just-in-time inventory. The most difficult aspect of implementing these improvement methodologies was the profoundly different way they viewed the role of quality in the process of manufacturing and the significantly different way that management and employees needed to work together to make improvements (Dobyns and Crawford-Mason 1991; Harry and Schroeder 2000). It was in these structures, relationships, and ways of working that American manufacturing struggled to reconcile itself to what the Japanese and Motorola had done. Ishikawa's quality circles as a way to bring workers together to discuss work problems and make improvements were very different from the processes employed at unionized General Motors in Detroit. It was an arduous journey for American manufacturing to finally look itself in the eye and admit that the real difference was not Japanese culture or demographics, but rather the Japanese were dead serious about eliminating waste and producing quality. They worked at it every day like their lives depended on it. In fact, they believed that their work lives did depend on it.

Looking deeply into the soul of American healthcare, it is hard to find a desperate drive to produce world-class quality and earth-shattering efficiency. Healthcare seems to be in the same state of confusion today that American manufacturing experienced in the 1980s when Japan tried to take over the world. The constant comparison of American healthcare to foreign countries and the relentless analysis that shows quality and costs significantly worse in America than almost anywhere else are very similar to the past for American manufacturing. During that period, American manufacturing was looking for the key to how Japan was doing it. What was the secret that made them so good at manufacturing when in the not-too-distant past, they created junk?

Since 1999, the Institute of Medicine issued report after report on the need to change American healthcare. The latest in 2012 took off the gloves and essentially said that American healthcare was wasting $750 billion annually, and it was time that this protected industry play by the same rules as any other industry. The Patient Protection and Affordable Care Act (PPACA), which became a law in

March 2010, created a number of initiatives designed specifically as shock therapy for American healthcare in the form of penalties for excessive costs or poor quality. It appears that the rules have changed (Office of Legislative Counsel 2010).

The PPACA included a number of provisions designed to incentivize American healthcare to improve quality and reduce costs. Lowering Medicare reimbursement, the act created accountable care organizations with upside and downside risk models to encourage healthcare to learn to manage costs and care. The new insurance exchanges and mandatory insurance programs held out the hope that hospitals might see fewer uninsured charity cases arriving in the emergency department.

A subtle but profound change occurring in American healthcare that could be the strongest driver for industrial quality is the shift from employer-paid, full-coverage healthcare insurance to high-deductible insurance plans. The employer-sponsored health insurance that grew into the primary method for paying for healthcare during and after World War II cost the employees nothing and paid for everything. In 2014, however, high-deductible employer-sponsored healthcare plans will be the only option for many workers (Galbraith et al. 2011; Bernard 2014). The plans require workers to pay thousands of dollars for healthcare services before their healthcare insurance begins to offer a coinsurance. Since businesses and their insurers failed to find a way to keep the costs of healthcare from rising faster than their companies' profits, they decided to unleash American consumers. Putting the burden on the employee who is purchasing the care makes the consumer the juggernaut of healthcare cost controls. If there is anything that will awaken a desperate desire to reduce costs and improve quality in American healthcare, it is confronting the American consumer and trying to make them pay for care in a healthcare system born out of insurance. Self-pay in American healthcare parlance is the same thing as charity care. Between the federal government penalties and the high-deductible health plans, American healthcare is finally facing the equivalent of the Japanese invasion of the 1980s.

Given this background, the momentum behind industrialization would seem to be real, and more hospitals and healthcare organizations will implement industrialization in the form of Lean and Six Sigma. The initial step in the process has often been, as it was in the National Demonstration Project in 1987, the application of quality improvement to nonclinical areas of hospitals. These areas are most like the industrial processes in that they involve the movement of supplies and the logistics of managing materials or the processes of cleaning rooms. These essentially mechanical processes lend themselves to industrial quality methods.

The real industrialization of healthcare, however, will occur when the medical staff, who have maintained the quasi-independence of their professional affiliations for over a century, cross the line and partner with the bureaucracy in healthcare organizations in working to improve quality and reduce costs. When the medical staff and the hospital bureaucracy join together, the debate will be over the medical staff's acceptance of the industrial definitions for quality improvement. The physician will no longer be the de facto customer of healthcare. The patient-customers will define value and waste in the processes, the goals of care, and the final determination of whether the value was worth the payment. Giving up personal preferences and prerogatives and stepping aside to invite the patient into the role of the real customer of healthcare will be tough, but it is the first step in industrialization.

This represents a significant change in the orientation not just for the medical staff but also for healthcare organization as a whole. As organizations move through the industrialization process and begin the journey to 21st century healthcare, the nursing staff and professional staff, the senior leadership, and the governing body or board all need training to understand the changes taking place. Industrialization that offers meaningful hope to improve quality and cost is very different from 20th century healthcare, and understanding this at all levels is important.

Nursing and other members of the healthcare team focus on the patients as the basis for what they do, but their training puts the emphasis on the practitioners and physicians to answer questions of the goals of care and what is valuable. Industrialization changes the conversations and requires patients to participate in ways that are very different from the past. Physicians determined value and waste in the care process in the past, but now these questions will go to patients. Working through the dynamics of these conversations takes time and slows processes until they become the norm.

Senior leaders will require training and reorientation on the new ways of leading and new ways of supporting processes defined by the patient-customers. As the implementation of Lean and Six Sigma moves forward, it requires high levels of engagement as everyone looks at their work and the goals of their work from new perspectives. The new ways of thinking about customers, value, waste, standardization, and the many other aspects inherent in industrial quality will cause a reordering of priorities and goals. A good example is within the financial bureaucracy of healthcare organizations, where the drive for quality and efficiency currently fights for priority with all the processes that continue to pay even though they represent bad care and excessive costs.

For the governing body, understanding and supporting the significant shift that occurs when patient-customers define value, waste, and the goals of care mean difficult conversations with physician leaders. In their interactions with physicians and healthcare leaders, they need to recognize how this will affect them and encourage and support the changes so that the organization can move forward. For physicians and other healthcare leaders in the organization, there are real questions as to whether patients are capable of this. At the same time, many patients will question why they have to do it.

Ultimately, industrialization is the way that American healthcare will improve. It is the only way to respond to the demands of consumers. American manufacturing needed new methods to meet the challenge of the Japanese, so American healthcare needs to industrialize to respond to their new patient-customers. What may not be obvious at first within American healthcare is that industrialization is not the end but a phase that leads to another type of healthcare.

As healthcare organizations pursue Lean and Six Sigma-level improvements in all areas of their organizations, including clinical care, the results of these efforts and all the changes they require bring another set of changes. These unexpected changes come from within American healthcare because of its unique development in the 20th century, and they point to a new type of healthcare system in the future. Industrialization generates changes in the values, structures, and processes of 20th century healthcare that result in the appearance of ten transitions that are the initial stages of the development of what will become 21st century healthcare. These transitions appear as the industrialization clashes with the assumptions that formed the basis for 20th century healthcare. Industrialization forces organizations to realize that the changes are not an addition to healthcare but a transformative force that is incompatible with the values, practices, and structures of 20th century healthcare. As industrialization displaces the healthcare of the past, new images of healthcare in the future appear. These new images challenge 20th century healthcare during industrialization, and they produce the ten transitions that lead to the future.

In addition to the specific actions required to implement industrial quality methods such as Lean and Six Sigma, another change that contributes to the appearance of the ten transitions is the development in healthcare organizations of extensive computerized information networks. Many people have viewed healthcare organizations and healthcare in general as complex systems for a number of years. In reality, the implementation of new information systems in healthcare organizations creates the networks of employees that make the complexity of healthcare a reality. This complexity emerges out of the interactions of networked individuals throughout the organization. These interactions and the common mission and values that the participants share form the basis for the creation of the organization moment by moment. The availability of data about the organization on a continuous basis contributes to the complexity, and the complexity is integral to the appearance of the ten transitions that emerge out of the combination of industrialization and the extensive computer networks.

Chapter 7

Industrialization Assessment

As healthcare organizations begin industrialization, recognizing strengths and weaknesses for the journey can be useful in determining what to do to support the significant changes that occur during this part of the journey to 21st century healthcare. Much that occurs in this process, however, occurs in conversations and discussions about industrialization and its effects on different groups that make it hard to assess progress. It is possible to identify certain aspects of industrialization as indicative of progress and to evaluate these on a regular basis.

The industrialization assessment is one tool to use to evaluate progress in some of the fundamental aspects of industrialization. It identifies specific groups and activities representing industrialization and provides a five-point scale to evaluate progress the organization is making in each area. Each assessment element identifies specific areas, and the total provides an overall view of the industrialization effort (see Figure 7.1).

The industrialization methods specifically addressed are Lean/Six Sigma since these are the two methods that are most easily understood and most frequently used. Lean and Six Sigma offer the advantage of specifically focusing on the key factors of customer, value, waste, product, flow, customer specification, data analysis, and standardization that are at the heart of the industrialization process for 20th century American healthcare.

Four groups are identified in the assessment as particularly important for assessing progress in industrialization in a healthcare organization. The four groups are the medical staff, nurses, senior leadership, and the board. These groups represent the most problematic and most important people to engage in industrialization and to ensure that they are involved in the process. The tool evaluates each of the groups based on four aspects of their involvement in industrialization. For each of the groups, the four aspects are support for Lean/Six Sigma, knowledge of Lean/Six Sigma, training in Lean/Six Sigma, and participation in Lean/Six Sigma improvements. These aspects require judgment on the part of the one doing the assessment, but the evidence to support these judgments should not be difficult to identify. The tool assesses the level of

51

52 ■ *Mapping the Path to 21st Century Healthcare*

Industrialization assessment		Weak 1	2	3	4	Strong 5	Ratings
Medical staff	Support for Lean/Six Sigma						
	Training in Lean/Six Sigma						
	Knowledge of Lean/Six Sigma						
	Participation in Lean/Six Sigma improvements						
Nursing	Support for Lean/Six Sigma						
	Training in Lean/Six Sigma						
	Knowledge of Lean/Six Sigma						
	Participation in Lean/Six Sigma improvements						
Senior leadership	Support for Lean/Six Sigma						
	Training in Lean/Six Sigma						
	Knowledge of Lean/Six Sigma						
	Participation in Lean/Six Sigma improvements						
Board	Support for Lean/Six Sigma						
	Training in Lean/Six Sigma						
	Knowledge of Lean/Six Sigma						
	Participation in Lean/Six Sigma improvements						
Patient-customer	Identification						
	Engagement (VoC)						
	Specifications as goals						
	Value identification						
	Waste elimination						
	Flow recognition						
	Product identification						
	Process standardization						
	Push/pull						
	Incremental innovation						
Tools	Project charter						
	SIPOCPCV						
	Flowchart						
	Value stream						
	Cause and effect/RCA						
	A3						
	5S						
	Plan-do-study-act						
	Six Sigma/Lean DMAIC						
	Statistical data analysis						
	Financial impact calculation						
	The constraint theory (Goldratt)						
Totals							

Figure 7.1　Industrialization assessment.

engagement with these four important groups. Support for Lean/Six Sigma evidenced by discussions as well as actions in the meetings provides information on progress in these four groups. Documentation in training in Lean/Six Sigma contained in training records, online and meeting education, and other ways demonstrates their involvement in educational activities. It is also a reminder of the importance of providing education to these groups to prepare them for making decisions, evaluating progress, and participating in Lean/Six Sigma. Knowledge of Lean/Six Sigma through simple evaluations following training or other assessments of competency offers a relatively easy means for determining the adequacy of the training. Participation in Lean/Six Sigma improvements looks for the level of engagement and involvement in the actual work of improvements by the four groups. This involvement is whatever is appropriate in the organizations for these groups such as reviews by the board or direct participation by nurses and physicians but should be sufficient that the groups are meaningfully involved in the industrialization process.

The assessment after the key groups is the patient-customers and their involvement in establishing the various aspects of Lean and Six Sigma improvement. The first step involves identifying the specific patient-customer groups associated with improvements. Identifying the pertinent patient-customers is a very significant aspect of industrialization. This requires the organization and the people involved in improvement to step away from the customer concepts of the past and to search out the specific patient-customers that are needed in the improvement.

Though there may be intermediate customers in a process that needs improvement, industrialization for 20th century American healthcare must focus on the needs of patient-customers even when they are not the direct recipient of the particular service or process. Every process in healthcare can be associated with patient-customers, and this is important as a corrective for healthcare's tendency to see its own internal needs as primary. The patient-customer is the ultimate beneficiary of the services and the final evaluator of healthcare processes. Learning to look beyond the proximal end of the process to the final patient-customer serves to prevent the definitions for value and waste and the goals of the process from getting tied up in the internal healthcare processes of professionals rather than focusing on the needs of the patient-customers. The historical tendency to focus on the internal issues of the healthcare organizations is a handicap to the efforts to improve in a way that really benefits the patients.

After identifying the patient-customers, their engagement in the improvement becomes a critical test of the effectiveness of the organization's industrialization. If the patient-customer as the voice of the customer (VoC) is not directly or only marginally involved, then the organization's effort to identify the other elements necessary for the improvement process becomes problematic. The strength or weakness of the involvement with patient-customers indicates the ability of the organization to progress with industrialization. A strong process will mean that the organization has arranged direct involvement by patient-customers in the improvement efforts.

The specification goals relate to the operations associated with a process. Identifying the goals that are required for each of these operations and meeting these specifications for all of the operations and improving these mean elimination of the defects and waste. Patient-customers provide these specifications as appropriate. Meeting these specifications contributes to the improvement of the overall goal.

Determining value is the basic focus of Lean/Six Sigma in any process improvement. Value means valuable to the patient-customer. It is something the patient-customer wants to purchase at an acceptable price. The organization needs to eliminate anything that the patient-customer does not value or want to purchase if possible. By looking to the patient-customers for the definition of value, the industrialization process shifts the improvement efforts away from its own internal concerns and focuses on the patient-customers who purchase the services or products.

The concept of value as what the patient-customer is willing to pay for or purchase has been problematic for healthcare organizations. Healthcare financial structures obscure sources of payment and the connection between payment and the patient-customer. By ensuring that the determination of value in the process comes from the patient-customer, healthcare organizations realign themselves with the ones that they need to serve and that will ultimately pay them in the future.

Waste elimination as a key aspect of Lean is particularly difficult in healthcare because the processes and facilities function so poorly that it becomes difficult to see the waste. Walking is a perfect example of Lean waste in healthcare that is invisible. Walking is fundamental to nursing practice primarily because the facilities used to deliver care are designed with long halls of rooms. Nurses walk continuously. Viewing walking as waste in most organizations is tantamount to saying that all nursing is waste. Healthcare's blindness to its own processes equates walking with essential activities, and this must change in order to reduce the waste in healthcare processes and activities.

Flow, like waste, is hard to see in most healthcare environments because the concept of flow was born out of the one-piece environment of manufacturing in which the continuous flow of individual pieces is more efficient than batching. In healthcare, flow associated with the clinical condition of patients is invisible when the flow of the patient is the change in the patient's condition. The ability to equate physiologic improvement with the progression of the patient toward discharge is an important translation of flow to healthcare.

Product identification represents a particularly challenging area for healthcare in the process of industrialization because the product is often the patient. In identifying the product created by the care process, the ability of the staff and the organization to view the patient as the product actually adds an important element to understanding the implementation of industrialization. The product for manufacturing is material that is modified or changed in fit, form, or function, and the customer recognizes it as value. When applied to patient care, the definition shifts specifically to the patient-customer as the product and what he/she considers valuable.

Process standardization represents one of the most important aspects of Lean/Six Sigma that has troubled healthcare from the initial attempts at using industrial improvement techniques. Standardization of a process requires that everyone involved in the process recognize the value of doing the process according to best practice the same way every time. Unfortunately for healthcare, professional judgment and often the personal preferences of individuals trump best practice and standardization. For this reason, very few processes in healthcare are well designed, and even fewer are performed the same way every time even in high-risk areas such as operating rooms and critical care areas. This situation has its roots in the professionalization of healthcare and the role of professionals in defining tasks.

In the flow of healthcare, pull and push relate to the relationships between the participants in the process and the flow of the process. Since waiting and delays are non-value-added steps in processes for the patient-customers, the patient's needs pull value when the patient transfers to the next step in the care process as soon as the patient is ready. Push occurs when the patient is ready to move and transfers to the next step in the process, but the next step is not ready for the patient. For patient-customer transfers, push occurs when the emergency department is full, and patient-customers arrive in patient care units prior to the units requesting the transfer. Optimally, pull occurs when the patient units call for patients from the emergency department because they have beds, and patients transfer as quickly as possible to the units. Within the context of flow, the value-added step is the transfer of the patient when the patient is ready to move, and the units signal their readiness to receive the patient-customer.

Innovation is an essential aspect of continuous improvement within the context of industrialization. Organizations should design all processes to correspond to the best practice and standardize it wherever process occurs. Once standardized, however, the people working in the process should begin to look for innovations that improve the process beyond the existing practice. This continuous innovation of standardized processes is not often a part of the work of employees in healthcare but represents a key concept for Lean/Six Sigma.

The need for innovation often arises out of the interactions between the staff and the patient-customers. As patient-customers change, the process also needs to change in response to their needs. By identifying the interaction with patients as the source of adaptive innovation, the organization focuses on the patient-customer rather than the desires of the leadership or the professionals. The ability of the organization to promote and support incremental innovation of processes is a valuable aspect of continuous improvement. Part of the reason that this method of supporting improvement does not occur more frequently is that it requires support and active involvement of middle management to promote innovation, support the employee's effort to improve, and encourage leadership to accept the innovation.

There are specific tools and techniques associated with Lean/Six Sigma that should be familiar with anyone involved in industrialization. The initial tool that is useful is the project charter as a defining document of an improvement initiative. The project charter identifies the people involved, the background for the current situation, and the rationale for improvement. It documents reporting time frames and milestones.

SIPOC is the acronym for supplier–inputs–process–outputs–customers that are part of a particular work process. This document assists the team in identifying all aspects of the process that may lie beyond the specific areas that are being improved. Including the supplier and inputs as well as the outputs and customers expands the ability of the team to recognize when these peripheral elements are integral to the improvement. An addition to the SIPOC is the patient-customer value (PCV) produced through each aspect of the supplier to customer flow.

Simple flowcharting brings the process to life as it creates a graphic of the invisible steps that make up the activities involved in the work. Since most work processes in healthcare have no material existence but actually exist only within the minds of the people involved, the creation of a graphic depiction of the steps that they go through makes it easier for them to realize what they are doing and helps others to understand it as well.

Value stream mapping elevates flowcharting to a higher level by adding the determination of value in the assessment of the steps of the process. If the steps add value that the patient is willing to pay for, it makes sense to consider them value-added steps. If they do not, then they are non-value-added steps and should be eliminated if at all possible. The most common non-value-added step in healthcare is waiting or delays. It is, again, in this area that healthcare struggles because so much of the care process incorporates waiting and delays as a routine part of the process. This is due to a variety of factors, but a key factor is the availability of physicians to make decisions, give orders, or sign paperwork to enable the patient to progress in the care process. When organizations recognize waiting and delays as non-value-added steps and take them seriously, significant progress in the overall flow of patients through healthcare organizations will occur.

Looking beneath the surface of a process can be difficult with all the activities of the people involved. The cause-and-effect diagram provides a way for individuals and groups to explore the root causes of process breakdowns and problems. This form of root cause analysis (RCA) facilitates inquiries in the form of asking "why" multiple times to arrive at the system issues. Though simple in design and easy to use, the ability to see the potential causes of problems and to seek for deeper system correlations can be powerful tools for improving processes that otherwise seem intractably problematic.

The Japanese, looking for ways to simplify the process of monitoring and reporting on improvements, used the A3-sized paper. This 11 × 17-in paper is large enough to contain sufficient information to enable someone unfamiliar with the project to quickly understand the background, the goals, the milestones, and progress that has been made. The typical A3 includes sections specifically for the important elements and often includes graphics of the processes.

To be such a powerful method for improvement, Lean often incorporates the simplest of ideas. Like a parent encouraging his/her children to clean their room, the 5S technique of sort–straighten–shine–standardize–sustain offers an easy way to change a chaotic storage area into an efficient distribution center for supplies or work. This technique points to the profound reality of industrialization that the effect of making work easier to perform with less waste through relatively simple changes is multiplied thousands of times and ultimately produces significant improvement.

Plan–do–study–act (PDSA) began with Shewhart and Deming and remained a part of the improvement environment through the years. It offers a simple, systematic method for conducting improvement that is easy to understand and use. For most people, the method is similar to the way they naturally make improvements, and they can follow it intuitively.

DMAIC is the acronym for define–measure–analyze–improve–control that grew out of early Motorola success at improvement and has been associated with Six Sigma from that time. DMAIC provides a structure for managing improvement projects that are either Six Sigma or Lean. Using the structure, a variety of improvement tools fit into each of the stages to facilitate the particular parts of the improvement efforts. Project Charter and SIPOC are frequently a part of the define stage. Measure brings in the data collection steps and can include qualitative or quantitative data in the form of numerical samples, value stream mapping, VoC surveys, and customer critical to quality. Analyze brings together the data analysis techniques of control charts, cause and effect, Pareto charts, and cost analysis. Improve involves the specific activities to improve the process including the PDSA cycles, force field analysis, flowcharting future state, and design of experiments. Finally, control focuses on standardizing the improvements through policies, procedures, and monitoring.

Statistical data analysis is more often associated with Six Sigma than with Lean, but it is an important part of industrialization because it grounds improvement in process data. Beginning with Shewhart's work with control charts, the use of statistical analysis of samples from the manufacturing process has been a key aspect of industrial quality control and quality improvement. For many hospitals, this is one of the most difficult aspects of improvement particularly as it relates to actual work processes because the data are not readily available, and the staff is unfamiliar with interpreting data. In the future, however, the ability of staff to understand statistical data related to process operations and to use that data to make improvements will be a fundamental part of everyone's work because improvement will be a part of everyone's job.

In the same way that statistical data have been a difficult part of improvement for healthcare organizations, financial impact analysis has been even more difficult. For most hospitals, the lack of financial information in the form of costs and revenues in real time has made the idea of reducing costs counterintuitive. It is difficult to correlate work processes with costs if the costs are unavailable until months after the departure of the patient. The infamous chargemaster offers insights into healthcare finances because the charges are not so much related to the costs of delivering care as they are to obscure interpretations of insurance contracts and governmental reimbursement. The lack of transparency in terms of cost for the staff inside the healthcare organizations is matched only by the lack of transparency for patient-customers who are seeking low-cost, quality healthcare. This will change in the future as the need to reduce costs places a premium on staff recognizing costs and patient-customers having access to information to make decisions on purchasing services.

Finally, Eliyahu M. Goldratt's (North River Press, 1999) *Theory of Constraints* has become an important part of the industrialization process for anyone trying to understand how to improve the movement of materials or patients through systems. By identifying system constraints as limiting flow and pointing to the need to optimize constraints in order to improve flow, Goldratt opened a new perspective on the reasons systems fail.

MAPPING YOUR ORGANIZATION'S TRANSITION TO 21ST CENTURY HEALTHCARE

Chapter 8

Transition Groups: Organizational, Process, and Cultural

As industrialization in the form of Lean and Six Sigma or another methodology makes steady inroads into healthcare organizations to reduce costs and improve quality, ten transitions will emerge out of the clash between the 20th century and the industrial phase to mark the beginning of 21st century healthcare. The ten transitions originate in the 20th century aspects of healthcare organizations, but they point to the future development of 21st century healthcare. As the implementation of industrialization expands, healthcare organizations will see the 20th century fading and the 21st century becoming clearer.

The ten transitions that lead to 21st century healthcare fall into three groups: organizational, process, and cultural. Within each group, there are several transitions that relate to specific aspects of healthcare and represent the changes from 20th to 21st century healthcare. Each of the transitions consists of a continuum. One end of the continuum represents an aspect of 20th century healthcare, and the other end represents that aspect as it may appear in 21st century healthcare. Movement of organizations results from progress away from the 20th to 21st century end of the continuum. Movement in the transitions reflects the assessment of characteristics pertaining to either the 20th or 21st century. As the characteristics of the organizations reflect more of the characteristics associated with the 21st century, they advance along the continuum toward the 21st century end.

Within the organizational transitions, there are four individual transitions: structure, relationship, leadership, and innovation. The structure transition reflects the internal dynamics of the way healthcare organizations are changing their organizational structures to adapt to industrialization and changes in healthcare as a service. In the relationship transition, the focus is on the changes between the organizations and the people they employ. Changes in healthcare require employees to view their work differently and for organizations to reevaluate

61

the relationships that exist with their employees. The nature of organizations and work will be different in 21st century healthcare. The leadership transition focuses on the implications for traditional positional power and the nature of leadership as healthcare moves from the 20th to 21st century. This transition relates to the nature of leadership and the way it is understood in the organizations. Rather than a task allocated to particular positions, leadership is redefined for the 21st century in the way it is understood, who exercises it, when it appears, and how it functions in organizations. The final organizational transition is the innovation transition, which highlights the transformation of innovation from a responsibility associated with positional power in the organization to a global responsibility that is shared by everyone as an adaptive response to changes.

The organizational transitions encompass profound changes in American healthcare. It is not surprising, however, that healthcare organizations would experience significant changes in their structure, leadership, organizational relationships, and innovation processes in light of the differences between the 20th century and modern industrialization. Due to its self-imposed insulation from the rest of the American economy and marketplace, healthcare retained significant aspects of the values, structures, and practices of the early 20th century even as it embraced the technology of the 21st century. This was evident in the 2012 Institute of Medicine report that essentially blasted American healthcare as completely out of touch with the current environment and creating excessive costs and poor quality as a result (IOM 2012).

Reflecting on the four transitions in the organizational group, the common theme is the movement away from the centralized structure of the early 20th century corporation as exemplified by the hierarchical organization chart to a much more diffused and complex organizational configuration. This new 21st century configuration represents an adaptation to the effects of the new electronic information systems in healthcare organizations and the increased demands at the point of contact between the organization and the new patient-customers. As the demands for information and services proliferate with the emergence of the new patient-customers, and as information moves faster through the organization between individuals and groups, the center organizational structures will not be able to maintain themselves as relevant and engaged if they retain the structure and practices of the 20th century. As the complexity increases with the multiplicity of interactions between employees and patient-customers, the decision making, leadership, creativity, and role of development will all migrate from the center to the outer edges, and the organizations will create themselves in new ways to meet the demands of the 21st century.

The second group of transitions is the process transitions. The production method transition tracks the change from the individual professional as the craftsman customizing care for patients to the multidisciplinary team that draws together many disciplines available today in a coordinated effort to provide patients with a full spectrum of services to meet their needs. This transition speaks directly to the new position of the physician within healthcare processes as a member of this new healthcare team process. The delivery system is the second process transition, and it addresses the shift from the hospital-based and relative limited services of the past to the multiplicity of services and service providers that are transforming healthcare in the 21st century. For patient-customers, the delivery system of healthcare has finally come to resemble the marketplace for other services offering many choices and a range of pricing options. The third transition is the information system transition, which highlights the profound changes resulting from the interconnectivity of information systems and the way this changes processes throughout healthcare. The fourth and final process transition is the financial transition. Along with the information system transition, this transition provides the foundation for the emergence of the patient-customers in the pursuit of quality and affordable healthcare. This is the reintroduction of the healthcare shopper into a new world of healthcare choices and pricing. As shoppers, patient-customers will transform American healthcare in their pursuit of what is valuable to them.

Within the process transitions, the overarching theme is the appearance of a vast network that encompasses healthcare organizations and the communities and universe within which they function. The electronic information network links together the expanding and diverse system of healthcare services and teams of healthcare professionals with the new patient-customers who have the power to choose their healthcare. As payers of healthcare abandon all hope of managing healthcare costs with healthcare providers, consumer health financing in the form of high-deductible insurance plans and health savings plans unleashes the dynamic force of people seeking quality healthcare at a price they can afford. Using the growing information systems and the growing diversity of services to meet the demands in the market, these patient-customers create their own virtual healthcare systems and in the process create 21st century healthcare in America.

The processes of care that were so carefully managed in the 20th century within the context of long-term relationships between patients and providers are completely overwhelmed as patient-customers seek out new services and new technologies that provide quality care at less costs. The structures of the past fade in the background as the disruptive factors of convenience and costs and good-enough quality enable patient-customers to obtain care within their own schedule and in the way that they choose. All of this brings about a new model of healthcare designed to operate within the 21st century.

The final group of transitions is the cultural transitions. The first cultural transition is the professional transition, which points to the profound change in the relationship between physicians and the hospital community that is occurring in the transitions. Once viewed as autonomous and singular in their knowledge and privileges, physicians within this transition become part of the overall healthcare process with a leading but not a solo voice. Their voice joins with a multitude of voices in the composition of patient care. The final cultural transition and the last of the ten transitions is the metaphor transition. The significance of the image of healthcare that patient-customers and the communities carry in their collective mind cannot be overestimated, and this transition draws attention to the movement from the blend of science and machinery that characterized the past to the complexity and adaptation that form the structure and nature of the healthcare system of the future.

The cultural transitions encompass the other eight transitions and provide the images that help to make sense of the amazing changes occurring in healthcare as it transitions to the 21st century. The 20th century image of the individual physician sitting by the bedside of the young patient and watching intently for the break in the illness disappears into the 21st century sea of professionals with a myriad of specialties blending together into a system of care in which no one reigns over the others. All the voices join together to speak and interpret the stories of the patient-customers, and each one adds an important part to the story.

Moving away from the scientific-machine image of the 20th century with its universe of precise laws, clear controls, and predictable outcomes, the image of the 21st century appears as a kaleidoscopic vision in which the colors change rapidly, and the many facets blend into surprising shades of light and color. This complex adaptive system of healthcare forms out of the needs of patient-customers and takes shape within the network of communications and interactions and services that are constantly evolving. It is in this future of healthcare that organizations will need the benefits of their industrialization and the vision of their transitions to succeed in meeting the needs of their patient-customers and communities.

Chapter 9

Transition Categories and Characteristics

As healthcare organizations progress in implementing industrialization, the conflicts between their 20th century heritage and the new values, structure, and practices of industrialization increase and become clearer. The conflict results from the introduction of industrialized quality and operational practices into this older system and the dramatic differences between the two. As this conflict intensifies, the ten transitions begin to appear. These transitions arise as the organizations recognize that the qualities and characteristics that are in conflict with industrialization actually come from the traditions of the 20th century values, structures, and practices that are embedded in the fabric of the organization's daily life. It is this realization that enables the organization to recognize that the new images are 21st century healthcare emerging out of the conflict between industrialization and 20th century healthcare.

The 21st century healthcare images that appear reflect the effects of the conflict but go beyond it. The healthcare of the 21st century is not an industrialized version of 20th century healthcare. It is also not healthcare converted to a manufacturing model. This new healthcare is evolving and dynamic and incorporates the influence of the history and the struggle of industrialization into a new configuration shaped by the needs, desires, and expectations of patient-customers who emerge out of industrialization as the new driving force in healthcare.

Though the process of industrialization began with the demands of employers, agencies, and the federal government for better quality and lower costs, it will result in a new American healthcare that responds to the needs of the new patient-customers of the future. For organizations to navigate this new 21st century healthcare, they need to recognize the ten transitions as the paths to this future. These paths only appear and become relevant as industrialization reaches the point that it truly challenges the aspects of 20th century healthcare that are deeply embedded in healthcare organizations. Their appearance and the ability of organizations to recognize the ten transitions and the images of the future they contain are an indication that industrialization has actually begun to change the essential nature of the organizations.

Once industrialization has reached the point that the ten transitions become relevant to the future of the organizations, the organizations need a way to monitor their progress in moving through the transitions. This progress does not reflect progress in industrialization but rather progress of the organizations in moving from 20th century healthcare to the creation of 21st century healthcare represented in the images of the latter. By the time the images of the 21st century become relevant and meaningful to the organizations, industrialization has reached an advanced stage. Up to this point, the organizations evaluated the strength of the various components of industrialization (industrialization assessment; see Chapter 7), but the real measure of the extent of industrialization is the organizations' awareness of the ten transitions and the relevance of the images of 21st century healthcare that they present.

Transition categories are useful in helping organizations to assess their progress within each of the ten transitions. The categories form the parameters of the transitions. There is a healthcare image in the 20th century category that reflects the essential nature of that aspect of healthcare as it appeared in the past in each of the ten transitions. An image of 21st century healthcare challenges the 20th century image in each of the transitions. These two images represent categories of what existed in the past and partially remains and what is in the future and is just beginning to appear. Movement away from the 20th century category and movement toward the 21st century images constitute progress in the transitions.

The origin of the categories for the 20th and 21st century is in the changes that are occurring internally in healthcare and in the environment within which healthcare functions. The most significant internal change is the early 21st century development of electronic information systems in healthcare organizations. This long-anticipated and feared apparition required healthcare organizations to give up their quaint paper medical records and physician processes. With funding from the federal government and the mandate for meaningful use of electronic information systems, healthcare organizations finally succumbed to the inevitable and to the enticement of federal funds and began the process of implementing these systems. Though problematic from the beginning, hospitals, physician practicers, and other healthcare organizations worked through the issues of moving from isolated computer systems in individual departments or practices to networked systems in the first decade of the 21st century.

The most significant external change that shapes the categories is the emergence of the patient-customer as a force in healthcare. Though forced into existence by the failure of 20th century healthcare to effectively address its quality and cost issues, the arrival of the patient-customer is transformative. The role of the patient as a customer in healthcare disappeared in the insurance structure of the middle and late 20th century. Medicare, Medicaid, and employer-sponsored insurance essentially bypassed the patient as a customer by taking the financing away from individuals and transferring it to the insurance companies and the government. This transference was a financial change that did not include a strong quality component designed to address the potential for healthcare organizations and their affiliated industries to abuse their roles in order to maximize their earnings. With no true customer functioning in healthcare and with no effective quality and cost programs, healthcare did what capitalists always do when given the opportunity; it maximized its profits by creating a medical–technological mass production machine with minimal quality restraints.

After years of increasing costs and declining quality as technology grew and consumption followed, the healthcare system became an intolerable burden on the employers and the government. The disciplining force of late 20th century industrial quality became the last hope for the runaway production system of American healthcare. Unfortunately, the power of healthcare proved resistant, and the voluntary implementation of industrial quality proved too slow to make a significant difference in costs and quality. Frustrated by the slow changes occurring in healthcare, employers and the government arbitrarily shifted the cost of healthcare to the patients in the form of high-deductible health insurance plans and reductions in Medicare coverage. Though frequently packaged as giving employees greater choice and minimized by employers and insurers in terms of its effect on consumers, the shift of significant healthcare costs back to patients set in motion many of the changes that are generating the categories of the 21st century that appear in the transitions.

Other changes coming out of these two very significant changes contribute to the development of the categories that frame the ten transitions. As the information systems expand and become more sophisticated, they create connections throughout organizations that increase the speed and frequency of interactions between employees and patient-customers even as they minimize the ability of the organization to monitor and manage the operations. This brings about changes in the structure, relationships, leadership, and innovation in the organization.

New demands placed on healthcare organizations by the newly empowered patient-customers generate changes in the organizations. Demand for services that deliver quality at lower cost and with greater convenience begin to disrupt the traditional hospital and physician configuration of 20th century healthcare. Technological development in healthcare that once focused on high-cost equipment for hospitals shifts to the development of devices that enable patients to manage more of their care at home with only minimal assistance. Financing arrangements become more flexible as healthcare becomes another charge item for families with reductions in insurance coverage. Finally, the pursuit of cost savings shifts the attention of patients as healthcare shoppers from higher-cost physician specialists to the more convenient and lower-cost providers who can address a wide range of care issues.

Taken together, the transformative effects of the new information systems and the empowerment of patient-customers set in motion many of the changes that shape the 21st century categories of the ten transitions. These categories are set over against the existing images of the 20th century that came into sharp relief as industrialization began to move through healthcare organizations and challenged the status quo that developed over the past century. In this way, the past and the future come together as two ends of a continuum that serve as the paths for healthcare as it moves into the future.

Within the organizational transition group, the structure transition contains the categories of 20th century hierarchy at one end of the continuum and 21st century complex system at the other. In the relationship transition, the 20th century transactional category forms one end of the continuum, and the emergent category forms the 21st century end. The leadership transition has control as the 20th century category and trust as the 21st century end of the continuum. The final organizational transition is the innovation transition, which begins with the 20th century centralized innovation category and ends with the 21st century adaptive innovation category.

Within the process transition group, there are also four individual transitions. The production method transition continuum begins with the 20th century craftsman category and ends with the 21st century multidisciplinary team category. The delivery system is the second process transition, and it begins with the hospital at the 20th century end and the continuum of care at the 21st century end. The third is the information system transition. This transition moves from the 20th century category of isolation to the 21st century network. The fourth transition is the financial transition. In this transition, we move from the 20th century fee-for-service category to the 21st century consumer health financing.

Within the cultural transition group, there are two transitions. The first cultural transition is the professional transition with autonomy as the 20th century category and integration as the 21st century category. The final transition is the metaphor transition. The metaphor transition begins with the scientific machine metaphor for the 20th century and the complex adaptive system as the category for the 21st century.

In the transitional assessment charts, organizations identify the characteristics or descriptive phrases for those characteristics associated with the transition that reflect the 20th century and list them under the 20th century category. In the same way, the 21st century category is at the top of the column for identifying characteristics that reflect the 21st century category images. These characteristics appear as industrialization progresses in the organizations and are listed in the chart. These form the images that help the organization and their employees to recognize the beginning points of the transition and the endpoints for their transitions. Though the categories are the same, the specific characteristics may differ in different organizations because the organizations reflect the diversity of the different customs, values, and practices of their communities. Examples of organizational characteristics for each category are included in the transitional assessment charts for each of the transitions in the following chapters to help leaders in identifying the characteristics in their organizations.

The characteristics become the beginning and end of the continuums for each of the transitions. They identify the characteristics of the 20th century and the vision of the 21st century for their organizations. Using these characteristics, the organizations have an opportunity to assess their progress along the continuums in articulating and promoting a clear vision of the future. The transitions help their organization to recognize the characteristics of the past that they are leaving behind and the vision of the future that they are pursuing. The value of mapping movement along the continuum is in motivating the people in the organization to see the future in the characteristics of the transition and work to move the organization toward their new future in healthcare. Identifying the characteristics is an important part of the organizations' engagement with the transitions and a way in which leadership, employees, and others recognize what was in the past that is fading and what will be in the future that is beginning to appear. Recognizing, documenting, and using the characteristics for each transition enable organizations to move toward the future that they believe awaits actualization.

The process for identifying the characteristics will be different depending on the particular transition and period that is in question. For the organizational transitions of structure, leadership, relationship, and innovation, the 20th century characteristics will be part of the senior leadership experience for individuals and groups who were present in the past and can recount their experiences. Asking these individuals and groups to identify what they believe has changed with the industrialization of the organization can help to identify characteristics that are beginning to fade. In the same way, leadership will need to assess new and/or different conflicts with what existed previously as the process for identifying the 21st century characteristics that may be in their initial stages. Recognizing the images of the past that are fading and the images of the future that are appearing as characteristics is the basis for the organization in identifying progress toward 21st century healthcare.

In the process transitions, the characteristics associated with production methods, delivery systems, information systems, and finance will be more objectively visible than the organization transitions. The 20th century history of process transitions will be documented in a variety of reports or work processes that are familiar to many people and can be recalled or researched. In a similar fashion, the 21st century future direction of these transitions may be evident at least in part in the organizations' plans, financial reporting, and future resource allocations. Bringing together this information will help to identify the characteristics that were part of the past and disappearing and those beginning to appear.

Perhaps the most subtle changes will be those associated with the cultural transitions that include professional and the overall organizational metaphor transitions. In searching for the signs of what existed in the past that characterize these two transitions, it will be helpful to survey people and groups who would have been present to see or notice the characteristics. A similar process could be used for characteristics associated with the future.

Professional status often appeared in the form of long white lab coats or other symbols of status. Individuals of particular clinical or administrative rank expected social deference and acknowledgment. The characteristics of 21st century healthcare would be similarly illustrated by the way that these symbols of autonomy and independence are no longer evident or that these individuals are incorporated into the organizations in new ways.

For the metaphors associated with organizations as a whole, the way people talk about the organization or the way they think it functions offers insights. Discovering the underlying metaphorical characteristics could require meetings and discussions with groups about the metaphors currently in use or referenced in the way people talk about the organization. In terms of the metaphors of the future, surveys and discussions with people on ways they see the organization changing or the way they see it responding to change as evidencing a particular image or concept portends the future metaphor that may be emerging.

Through the categories and characteristics of the transition assessment charts, the progress of healthcare organizations as they move from the 20th to 21st century in the ten transitions becomes clearer. Using a variety of techniques such as focus group discussions and surveys to discover the consensus within the organization of the characteristics that are most descriptive of the past and the characteristics that appear to be emerging for the future, the characteristics and the progress toward the 21st century healthcare organization can be assessed. This provides a means for healthcare organizations to recognize important internal and external changes as part of this progression. It also enables organizations to see the images that are appearing that offer insights into the future. Using these future images, the organization is able to guide and motivate its employees to strive to realize the future that awaits.

Chapter 10

Transition Assessment Tools

Assessing progress within the ten transitions begins with the transition assessment charts for each of the ten transitions. These charts contain two characteristic columns and two point columns. The charts consist of columns designated as 20th and 21st century, and each of these columns carries a label with the category appropriate to the transition and column. Each of the category columns has a column for points. The 20th century has a negative point column, whereas the 21st century has a positive point column.

In each of the columns, organizations list the characteristics for that particular category. In the 20th century column, the characteristics reflect the category for the organization as it was and may still be in the 20th century. In the 21st century column, the characteristics reflect the images of the organization for that category that are beginning to appear. Comparing the characteristics in the 20th and 21st century column, the characteristics are assessed, and a –1 is assigned when the characteristic that is most dominant reflects the 20th century, and a +1 is assigned when the characteristic that is most present in the organization reflects the 21st century. The totals for the point's columns are added up and the totals are entered at the bottom of each column. Identify five characteristics initially for each transition assessment chart column (see Figure 10.1).

Transferring the totals of the 20th and 21st century from each of the transition assessment charts to the transition scorecard provides a way to review the point totals for the ten transitions and to develop the final total for the transition progress scale. The scorecard also provides a comparison of the transitions to identify which are impeding progress the most and which have progressed the farthest. When the final number is transferred to the scale, the overall progress of the organization as reflected in the aggregate of all the ten transitions will be displayed for a particular date (see Figure 10.2).

Organizations begin at the center or zero on the transition progress scale. A larger negative number moves the organization toward the 20th century end of the scale and represents a lack of progress. A larger positive number moves the organization toward the 21st century and represents progress in adapting to the

20th century characteristics	Points (neg)	21st century characteristics	Points (pos)
Total (record on transition scorecard)		Total (record on transition scorecard)	

Figure 10.1 Transition assessment chart.

Transitions scorecard	20th century (neg. no.)	21st century (pos. no.)	Total (sum neg. and pos.)
Organizational structure: hierarchy to complex system			
Organizational relationship: transactional to emergent			
Leadership: control to trust			
Innovation: centralized to adaptive			
Production method: craftsman to multidisciplinary team			
Delivery system: hospital to continuum of care			
Information system: isolation to network			
Financial: fee-for-service to consumer health financing			
Professional: autonomy to integration			
Metaphor: scientific machine to complex adaptive system			
Totals (transfer sum to transition progress scale)			

Figure 10.2 Transition scorecard.

new healthcare model. A total of 50 points are possible in either direction based on the five characteristics that are identified for each of the ten transitions (see Figure 10.3). The overall mapping of the path to 21st century healthcare can be visualized as a flowchart (see Figure 10.4).

The illustration that follows provides an example of mapping the transitions. It begins with the transition assessment charts from each of the ten transitions. The organization lists the characteristics under the 20th and 21st century category and chooses the characteristics that currently describe the organization in that aspect. For the characteristics that describe the organization's current state, "1" is placed next to the characteristic, as shown in Figure 10.5.

The organization places the totals from each of the columns of the transition assessment chart in the correct columns and rows of the transition scorecard.

Transition Assessment Tools ■ 73

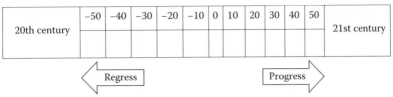

Figure 10.3 Transition progress scale.

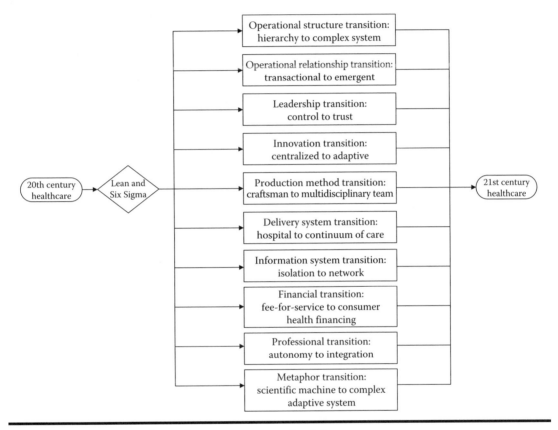

Figure 10.4 Mapping the path to 21st century healthcare.

20th century hierarchy	Points (neg)	21st century complex system	Points (pos)
Traditional organizational chart design with positional power highest at the top	1	Organization chart displaying organizational communication and functional support connections	
Accountability defined by vertical reporting relationships		Accountability based on response to needs to support work and connections across system	1
Information follows reporting design	1	Information flow supports work and connections across system	
Allocation of resources controlled by higher positions	1	Access to resources based on guidelines with few restrictions	
Department activities directed by higher positions	1	Work and support activities develop spontaneously in response to changes	
Total (record on scorecard)	−4	Total (record on scorecard)	1

Figure 10.5 Example—Organizational transition structure characteristics assessment.

74 ■ *Mapping the Path to 21st Century Healthcare*

The scorecard provides a quick review of all the categories and sums the values for all the ten transitions (see Figure 10.6).

The organization places the total sum from the transitions scorecard on the transition progress scale. With zero in the center, the left indicating movement toward the 20th century, and the right indicating movement toward the 21st century, the results indicate whether the organization moved toward the 20th or 21st century based on the transitions. The transition progress scale has an initial scale of 0–50 points on the right and 0–50 points on the left in gradations of 10 points. The organization can adjust the scale to a range that meets the needs for tracking its progress, as shown in Figure 10.7.

Transitions scorecard	20th century (neg. no.)	21st century (pos. no.)	Total (sum neg. and pos.)
Organizational structure: hierarchy to complex system	−4	1	−3
Organizational relationship: transactional to emergent	−4	1	−3
Leadership: control to trust	−5	0	−5
Innovation: centralized to adaptive	−3	2	−1
Production method: craftsman to multidisciplinary team	−5	0	−5
Delivery system: hospital to continuum of care	−1	4	3
Information system: isolation to network	−2	3	1
Financial: fee-for-service to consumer health financing	−4	1	−3
Professional: autonomy to integration	−3	2	−1
Metaphor: scientific machine to complex adaptive system	−4	1	−3
Totals (transfer sum to transition progress scale)	−35	15	−20

Figure 10.6 Example—Transitions scorecard.

Transition progress scale

Date:

20th century	−50	−40	−30	−20	−10	0	10	20	30	40	50	21st century
				X								

← Regress   Progress →

Figure 10.7 Example—Transition progress scale.

MAPPING THE TEN TRANSITIONS

Chapter 11

Organizational Transition: Structure—Hierarchy to Complex System

The first organizational transition is the structure transition (see Figure 11.1). This transition begins with the 20th century hierarchy category as the traditional way in which healthcare organizations viewed management and reporting relationships. The continuum of this transition ends with the 21st century complex system category that reflects the new structure of organizations appearing with the implementation of information technology and the relationships and interactions that arise out of this new capability for employees and patient-customers.

To use the structure transition assessment chart, identify five characteristics in your organization that fit the 20th century hierarchy category, and document them in the column. In the 21st century complex system category, identify five characteristics of complex systems in your organization that represent changes from the 20th century hierarchy characteristics. Using the transition assessment chart, identify the dominant characteristic of the 20th or 21st century currently in your organization, and assign a 1 in the column for that characteristic. When you have completed the assessment of the five characteristics in each category, total the columns, and document the totals on the transitions scorecard. The sum of the columns based on the comparison of the dominance of the characteristics indicates whether your organization reflects more the 20th or 21st century healthcare organization. In identifying characteristics of the 20th and 21st century organizational structures in your organization, there are a variety of sources of information that you can use. The organization chart, which is very common, provides valuable insights into the structure and management of the organization. It also offers the means for assessing the influence of information technology on the structures of your system.

The appearance of the original organization charts at the New York and Erie Railroad in 1854 and a very different organization chart at the Union Pacific and

77

20th century hierarchy	Points (neg)	21st century complex system	Points (pos)
Total (record on scorecard)		Total (record on scorecard)	

Figure 11.1   Organizational transition structure characteristics assessment chart.

Southern Pacific Railroads in 1910 illustrates the applicability of the organization chart for assessing characteristics of organizations and the effect of information technology on the structure of organizations. Daniel McCallum as the head of the New York and Erie Railroad "created the first organization chart in response to the information problem hobbling one of the longest railroads in the world" (Rosenthal 2013). At the time, according to Rosenthal, the telegraph was generating more information than the railroad employees could manage effectively, but it was information that was vital to prevent accidents when rail traffic moved in opposite directions on the same tracks. McCallum needed a way to organize the flow of information and decision making in the railroad. Rosenthal notes that McCallum's organization chart does not resemble the modern triangular chart with the highest authority at the top but instead resembles a tree with the board of directors and senior leadership at the root of the tree in support positions and division superintendents and departments as the branches. This configuration retained the operational decision making at the branches while permitting the flow of useful information from the branches to the trunk root (Rosenthal 2013).

In the 1870s, the Pennsylvania Railroad developed a different type of organization chart. This chart, popularized in *Railroad Administration* in 1910 as the organization chart of the Union Pacific and Southern Pacific Railroads to organize its 80,000 workers and 55,000 mi of rail and steamer lines, placed the board and president of the railroad at the top of the chart in the highest positions of power (Harvard Business Review [HBR] 2014). The chart "visualized the pathways by which the president of the railroad collected reports and recommendations from each branch, making strategic decisions atop the chain while each railroad was run independently" (HBR 2014, p. 32). With the various departments and positions displayed in boxes with reporting accountabilities, this chart established the common theme of modern organizational bureaucratic structure and reporting.

The changes that technology and complexity brought to the railroads as organizations led to the development of the two charts. McCallum developed his chart as a way to organize the flow of information at the operational level as new technology in the form of the telegraph made real-time information available up and down the tracks for the first time. He created a tree-like structure that shaped the flow of this real-time information to make it effective at the operational level (Rosenthal 2013). The Pennsylvania Railroad chart expanded by the Union Pacific and Southern Pacific Railroads created a design to illustrate the control and accountability by linking the departments to the positions of senior management. It did not address the flow of information between the various departments but rather between the departments and the top leaders in the structure (HBR 2014).

These two charts represent the two categories of structure transition. The Union and Southern chart exemplifies the hierarchical chart used by most health-care organizations during the 20th century and still used today. It identifies the highest-ranking positions at the top of the chart and links the departments that report to them. Its purpose is to describe the reporting and accountability that facilitate command and control in the 20th century bureaucratic design of organizations.

The McCallum organization chart comes much closer to expressing the health-care organization of the future though it appeared early in the 1850s. With the implementation of information technology, healthcare faces a situation similar to the arrival of the telegraph. For the first time, employees throughout health-care organization have access to real-time information about the patients and the operations of the organization. This new information technology pushes decision making to the fringes where the organization interfaces with its patient-customers. Information moving through the system promotes the development of the organization as a complex system and requires a structure based on communication that occurs with many individuals and groups interacting together and with patient-customers. The significant increase in the flow of information and the complexity of the organizations overwhelms the organizational structures of the past and pushes the organization to move from the older chart to a new structure that forms the characteristics in the organizational structure transition.

20th Century Hierarchy

As you begin your development of the organizational structure transition assessment chart, you need to identify five characteristics for the 20th century hierarchy category. Merriam-Webster Online Dictionary defines hierarchy as "a group that controls an organization and is divided into different levels" or "a system in which people or things are placed in a series of levels with different importance or status." In healthcare organizations, the hierarchical structure of management dominated the 20th century and continues today as reflected in most organization charts. The traditional chart with its boxes and lines exemplifies the scientific view of management and the pursuit of efficiency that were the hallmarks of industrial era and the 20th century.

Hierarchical organization charts often have positions at the top of the chart and departments below. The positions at the top, often beginning with "C" such as chief executive officer (CEO), chief financial officer (CFO), etc., identify the positions in the organization exercising authority over the departments that report to them. Lines with arrows show accountability between the positions and reporting departments. The positions at the top of hierarchical charts customarily have the most control and authority, and the power decreases progressively toward the bottom of the chart. Higher compensation, access to information, and status within the organization are associated in most organizations with higher levels on the chart.

The organization chart presents a structure designed to answer the question, "Who is in charge?" When anyone needs to know who is in charge or in control of particular areas or able to provide resources or direction to departments, the organization chart is the fastest way to obtain an answer to the question. It clearly sets out these power relationships in graphic form and so becomes a guide to the organization and the management and relationships that exist between positions and departments.

Once you have identified the hierarchical structure of the organization and indicated this as a characteristic in the transition assessment chart, documenting the effects that come out of this organizational structure provides the remaining characteristics as qualities that are part of 20th century healthcare organizations. The most common effects of this structure that may serve as characteristics under hierarchy for your organization relate to the reason the structure was developed historically. The four characteristics of hierarchy involve the use of positional power or power associated with the position on the organization chart to manage accountability, information flow, resources, and activities.

Five possible characteristics for the 20th century healthcare organizations under the organization structure transition are as follows: (1) traditional organizational chart design with positional power highest at the top; (2) accountability defined by vertical reporting relationships; (3) information follows vertical reporting design; (4) allocation of resources controlled by higher positions; and (5) department activities directed by higher positions.

Selecting these characteristics of the hierarchical structure as 20th century does not indicate a judgment as to whether these characteristics are bad or wrong. These characteristics of the hierarchical structure are common in 20th century healthcare organizations. The goal of the assessment is to determine which 21st century characteristics relate to these 20th century characteristics in order for the organization to determine how the 21st century may be different from the 20th century and to move toward the 21st century end of the continuum.

The importance of accountability defined in the chart captures the nature of the bureaucratic organization in the 20th century healthcare organizations or the way in which these organizations function. The particular departments or positions that are accountable to positions express the prioritization and the dominance of positions within the hierarchy of the organization. If nursing is a division depicted as accountable to a CFO with operational responsibilities, then this arrangement reflects the priorities of the financial division in ways that are different from nursing reporting directly to the CEO. The arrangement of positions and departments in terms of accountability makes the traditional 20th century organization chart and its presence and role in the organization very important in defining the organization as characterized by a 20th century structure.

Information flow is a possible characteristic in the 20th century structure chart that reflects the hierarchical organization. In 20th century organizations, the flow of information follows the vertical reporting relationships in the organization chart. It expresses the dependency of lower positions on higher positions to know what is happening and what to do in response to what is happening. Higher positions provide guidance to their departments to ensure the execution of the overall plan of the organization, and departments report their results to the higher positions.

The flow of information established by the hierarchy specifically relates to the use of position power to develop plans for the organization and communicate them down to the operational areas. The information flow up the chain of command provides senior leaders with information on the progress made in responding to the directives previously communicated. The structure specifically addresses the need for information to flow down from the higher positions and up from the departments but does not describe or facilitate the flow of information outside of the vertical structure.

Access to organizational information is a distinction that differentiates the higher and lower positions of the organization. Superiors communicate information about the overall strategy of the organization and the details of organizational planning only to the degree necessary to enable operational areas to fulfill their roles in accomplishing the plans. High positions manage information flow about the organization and their knowledge of this information in real time as important in establishing their position within the hierarchy and defining their role and significance to the organization and to the departments that report to them. The 20th century organization controls the ability of departments or individual employees to act independently or to know what is happening at an organizational level by keeping information flow carefully controlled within the positional power structure. This reinforces the dependency of departments on the higher positions and reduces the ability of operational areas and individuals from gaining enough information to act independently.

Positions at the top of the hierarchical organizational chart manage the allocation of resources as an essential aspect of the power that they exercise. Departments within the organization appeal to the positions that they report to for additional supplies, personnel, equipment, and other forms of resources and receive authorization or denial for those resources depending on the judgment of the positions above them. The control of resources represents a significant influence to the overall culture of the organization. The greater the control of resources and the more difficult the resources are to obtain, the greater the dependency and the more influence the positions of power at the top of the chart exert over their departments. The number of meetings, the prevalence of innovation, and the speed by which organizations adapt to their environment all relate to access to resources as well as information.

The final characteristic that may be associated with hierarchical structures relates to the activities of departments and the ability of positions at the top to manage and control these activities. For organizations structured hierarchically, the direction of activities by departments comes down from higher positions, and the reporting of the results of those activities goes up to the higher positions. This arrangement strengthens the ability of the higher positions to manage activities based on their knowledge about the overall plan for the organization and the control of the resources associated with those plans. The more tightly higher positions control the activities of their departments in performing work, developing new activities, and otherwise adapting to situations in real time, the more difficult it is for the departments to respond to changes.

21st Century Complex System

In the organizational structure transition, the 21st century structure category is the complex system. This organizational structure represents the future of healthcare organizations, and, as it appears, it serves as a guide in the move along the continuum of the organizational structure transition. The motivation to move away from the hierarchical structure of healthcare organizations to a complex system image comes from the implementation of electronic information technology that creates a new infrastructure in healthcare organizations. This infrastructure supports real-time information dissemination of operational and organizational information throughout organizations. The flow of information and the connections between individuals based on the new information technology serve as the foundation for the complex system and for the creation of a new structure of the organization that is different from the hierarchical structure of the past (Wheatley 1992; US DHHS 2012).

As healthcare organizations evolve as complex systems, the complex system attributes will appear and shape the nature of the organization. Emergence of new structures, patterns, and processes within the system occur unpredictably through the interactions of the individuals connected through the system (Zimmerman 2011). Connectivity in complex systems supports the relationship-centered way in which the systems relate internally and to the environment (Zimmerman 2011). Through these interconnections, the system self-organizes or creates a new order spontaneously without the intentional intervention of individuals or the central leadership (Zimmerman 2011). Smaller systems within systems or embedded systems operate simultaneously and coevolve over time (Zimmerman 2011). The design and management of the system are distributed, and simple rules serve to shape the functioning of the system (Zimmerman 2011).

Sophisticated information systems that link individuals within healthcare organizations shape the organization and the way it operates. The hierarchical structure of the past continues to influence the system but no longer has the capacity to control it as in the past. Individuals share information in real time and coordinate activities with less and less direction from the hierarchical structure. The emphasis is more on connections, communications, and relationships and less on positional power and titles and a defined hierarchy.

Five possible characteristics for the 21st century complex system under the organization structure transition are as follows: (1) organization chart displaying organizational communication and functional support connections; (2) accountability based on response to needs to support work and connections across system; (3) access to resources based on guidelines with few restrictions; (4) access to organizational information open and transparent; and (5) work and support activities develop spontaneously in response to changes. Beginning with the organization chart, as healthcare organizations move toward a complex system orientation, a redesign of the chart appears inevitable. This redesign needs to reflect the shift from dependence on the positions at the top of the organizational chart to reliance on the connections and relationships created by the new information technology infrastructure. As a complex system, healthcare organizations need to consider the ability of individuals and groups to share information and to create new processes and structures to manage changes in the organization and the environment without reliance on a central structure or positions of power. These changes occur as information becomes available in real time through information technology and groups' reaction to the information.

Given this situation, the depiction of the complex system is the more useful and accurate image of the 21st century healthcare organization and much more useful to anyone interested in how the organization functions. Positions continue to exist, but the nature of the power has shifted from positional power based on a vertical alignment to the relationships that represent the ability to deliver support because the focus has shifted to the interface between the organization and the patient-customers rather than the operations and central leadership. The ability to interact effectively with patient-customers and to obtain resources needed to respond to requests becomes the most important linkage in the complex system that now makes up the organization.

The second characteristic of the 21st century complex system is the shift from power or accountability structures aligned in a vertical configuration to the complex system of the 21st century healthcare organization that defines accountability based on functional responsibilities and interdependencies. Functions take the place of departments because the department names were limited in their ability to express what they actually did. Department names represented an older categorization rather than the actual function or operation of the area. The designation of departments such as physical therapy or nursing in the past no longer encompasses the broader range of services and activities in the future. Providing functional designations within the organizational chart and showing the connections to other functions create a clearer picture of the actual relationships and interdependencies that are part of the 21st century network. Mapping the connections between functions indicates the responsibilities to deliver the services to meet needs in the organization as other areas of the organization deliver services to meet the needs of patient-customers. Defining these relationships becomes critically important in helping the organization to recognize the interdependencies and to facilitate the delivery of services between departments that must work together to fulfill functions. These functional responsibilities define the relationships that exist to perform the important work of the organization.

Even as the functional relationships define the way that different areas in the organization relate to one another, the flow of resources takes on a greater significance in supporting the work of the various areas that depend on each other functionally and the patients and other customers that rely on the organization. The third characteristic of the 21st century complex system is access to resources based on guidelines with few restrictions that aligns with services to assist customers and responds to unusual circumstances that may occur. The connections within the complex system highlight the way the resources are allocated as they are needed through the system.

In this new configuration, the most prominent nature of the complex system is the information flow moving in many directions. No longer trapped in the vertical structure of the 20th century but now able to depict information flows as it exists in reality in the organization, the new organizational chart provides a visual depiction of the way information supports the relationships between functions and supports the delivery of services to customers. Power and accountability are in the capacity of various major functional areas to support those aspects of the system that directly interact with customers and deliver services rather than in a vertical alignment associated with the top of the chart. Information flow is the image that best defines the links between these areas of the healthcare organization and the relationships that they share in relation to the customer.

Even as the extent of information flow is the chief characteristic of the 21st century complex system, open access by staff and multidirectional flow of organizational information in real time are an important distinction between this new structure and the 20th century structure of healthcare organizations. Open access to organizational information, the fourth characteristic of the 21st century complex system, breaks down the silo configuration of the vertical alignments that required information to follow the power and control structure and delivers information about the organization to the functional areas that need it to develop responses. The functional areas and service delivery areas no longer have the time to wait for central leadership to receive, analyze, and develop a response to changes that are occurring inside the organization and in the surrounding environment. Changes are happening rapidly, and the speed of change requires rapid responses. Waiting for information to flow from the highest positions to the lowest areas of the organization compromises the ability of the individuals at the interface with customers to react effectively.

More importantly, this open structure transforms information from a symbol of power and control to the key to creating effective services for patient-customers by enabling service delivery and support functions to respond quickly. Whereas information about the organization was once considered a privilege, it is now viewed as necessary because of the role it plays in supporting the care of patients and responding to the needs of customers.

In the 20th century, change was something that appeared in the distance like a train approaching an organization. Management within the organization had time to ponder the changes, consider different responses, and deliberate on how to react. Individuals offered proposals in response to the anticipated changes. Finally, management reviewed all the recommendations and developed responses that considered all the various perspectives and stakeholders before developing the final response to the change.

In the 21st century complex system, the final characteristic for consideration is the alignment of accountability and information to support system responses to changes because this has become a matter of survival. In the new environment, accountability and information flow follow the paths of efficient and effective response to changes rather than the static structure of the past. Individuals who can respond to changes regardless of their positions access information and exercise the power to move forward in developing changes. Since change occurs unpredictably anywhere in the system, the confluence of information may enable a person at a lower level to produce responses more effectively than management. This ability of the healthcare organization to shift accountability to the point where there is knowledge and ability to act represents a major change from the structures of the past.

The 21st century complex system stands in stark contrast to the 20th century hierarchy and represents an image of the nature of healthcare in the future. Rather than an organizational chart based on power, control, and reporting structures as described by the Union and Southern Railway chart, the 21st century complex system presents a fluid, dynamic organizational structure in which the need for real-time information and rapid response and support forms the way in which the organization is structured and operates. The McCallum New York and Erie Railroad offers a prescient vision of the type of chart that better captures the new structure of American healthcare than the traditional organization chart. Rather than waiting for a response from the central leadership unaware of many of the changes occurring in the organization, speed dictates that action take place as quickly as possible at the point of care, the flow of information, and the accountability supporting this response. Functions support service delivery and the actual service delivery areas through sophisticated information systems to facilitate rapid changes and to maintain the

	20th century hierarchy	Points (neg)	21st century complex system	Points (pos)
	Traditional organizational chart design with positional power highest at the top		Organization chart displaying organizational communication and functional support connections	
	Accountability defined by vertical reporting relationships		Accountability based on response to needs to support work and connections across system	
	Information follows reporting design		Access to resources based on guidelines with few restrictions	
	Allocation of resources controlled by higher positions		Access to organizational information open and transparent	
	Department activities directed by higher positions		Work and support activities develop spontaneously in response to changes	
	Total (record on scorecard)		Total (record on scorecard)	

Figure 11.2   Example—Organizational structure transition characteristics assessment.

communication that enables resources to move quickly. It is in this environment that the demands of 21st century healthcare overwhelm the structures of the 20th century and require that they change, or the organization will fail. This is the motivation for movement along the continuum of the organizational structure transition (see Figure 11.2).

Chapter 12

Organizational Transition: Relationship—Transactional to Emergent

The second organizational transition is the relationship transition (see Figure 12.1). This transition begins with the 20th century transactional category as the traditional way in which healthcare organizations and employees viewed their relationship. The continuum of this transition ends with the 21st century emergent category that reflects a new perspective on organizational and employee relationships reflecting the nature of 21st century organizations and work as evolving. To use the relationship transition assessment chart, identify five characteristics in your organization that fit the 20th century transactional relationship category, and document them in the column. In the 21st century column, identify five characteristics that indicate a change from the 20th century transactional relationship to the 21st century emergent relationship. Using the transition assessment chart, identify the dominant characteristic from the 20th or 21st century currently in your organization, and assign a 1 in the column for that characteristic. When you have completed the assessment of the five characteristics in each category, total the columns, and document the totals on the transitions scorecard. The sum of the columns based on the comparison of the dominance of the characteristics indicates whether your organization reflects more the 20th or 21st century healthcare organization.

Frederick Taylor (1911), Frank Gilbreth (1914), and others in the early 20th century approached labor and organizations with the goal of applying science to management to achieve efficiency. By management defining all the parts of the work process, designing the way they were performed, and training the workers to follow specific steps, scientific management sought to create the most efficient method of performing work. Businesses hired workers, taught them to perform the work as designed, and compensated them for performing the work. It was not the workers' responsibility to change the work, only to perform it.

87

20th century transactional relationship	Points (neg)	21st century emergent relationship	Points (pos)
Total (record on scorecard)		Total (record on scorecard)	

Figure 12.1 Organizational transition relationship characteristics assessment chart.

The modern expression of this process is the transaction that occurs when a healthcare organization hires an employee. Merriam-Webster Online Dictionary defines a transaction as "a business deal or an occurrence in which goods, services, or money are passed from one person, account to another," and this captures the essential nature of 20th century healthcare employment. The employer provides a job description that defines the work as specific activities and the compensation the worker can expect for performing the work well. This job description also specifies the individuals or positions with authority over the worker. This document and the transaction by which the worker and the organization indicate agreement of the job description in exchange for the compensation establish the fundamental parameters of the relationship.

In the organizational relationship transition, the focus is on the nature of the relationship between the people who work in organizations and the management and culture of the organization. In the 20th century, the typical bureaucratic organizations defined the relationships based on the transaction in which the worker exchanged specific labor for a negotiated compensation offered by the organization. In the 21st century, healthcare organizations need different work and a different relationship with their workers because the complexity of the organization and the interactions with patient-customers require employees to go beyond specific tasks. No longer is it sufficient for the worker to agree to perform certain tasks in exchange for specific wages.

The 21st century healthcare organization as a complex system requires employees to operationalize the mission, vision, and values into the process of their work. This translation occurs as employees, patient-customers, and others interact thousands of times a day in hundreds of different situations. It is in these interactions and processes that employees actively create their roles as they participate in the creation of the organization and its culture through the ways that they operationalize the mission and values in their activities, words, and writing. Specific tasks enumerated in a job description as the sum total of a job no longer encompass the work or the needs of the organization. The relationship between the worker and the organization in the 21st century is an agreement on the mission of the work and the values that shape it. The organization needs the work and the role of the worker to emerge out of the multiple relationships, processes, and decisions that will occur each day. It is in this context that the continuum of the organizational relationship transition serves to evaluate progress toward 21st century healthcare.

20th Century Transactional Relationship

In the 20th century transactional relationship, the emphasis is on the way in which the employee and the organization establish the relationship. An agreement or transaction that encompasses the expectation by the organization of the work the employee will perform and the compensation the organization agrees to pay for the work—these two parties transact the agreement that establishes the nature of the relationship.

Five possible characteristics for the 20th century transactional relationship are as follows: (1) task-specific job description defines work and compensation; (2) evaluations focus on specific tasks; (3) job and work defined by management; (4) specific application of organization mission and values to the work is not defined; and (5) management modeling of mission and values inconsistent.

In the first characteristic of the 20th century transactional relationship, the job description defines the transaction between the worker and management in terms of work. It describes the work required to earn the specific compensation. This was the heart of the transaction for the work and the basis for the relationship with management. If the worker agreed to the terms, then they completed the transaction, and the expectations of the worker and management were met. For management, the work represented the time and effort of the employee in exchange for a set amount of money and benefits. This defined the relationship.

The second characteristic of the 20th century transactional relationship highlights the way in which management evaluated the work performed by the employee. Specific tasks included in the job description defined the work. As the experts, management designed the work and established the parameters for its execution. The employee fulfilled the tasks identified in the job description and followed the specific requirements established by management for the work. This included specific arrival and departure times and specific activities to be accomplished during the time. Management arranged training as needed and provided guidance to ensure that the worker understood the work.

In evaluating the work, management evaluated the specific tasks. Based on the job description and the record of the work, the worker's supervisor evaluated the number of tasks completed, any work with errors, and the worker's record of arriving on time and completing the specified tasks. If the worker performed the specific tasks well, the worker would receive a good evaluation and would perhaps receive a raise or a bonus. If the manager determined that the work was not done well, the worker might be fired or receive no increases. The specific tasks and the worker's record of accomplishing the tasks were the basis for the ongoing relationship.

In the third characteristic of the 20th century transactional relationship, the worker and management are distinct not only in their relationship concerning the work and the compensation but also in terms of decisions. Management expects the worker to perform the work and fulfill all the requirements defined for the position. Changing those requirements or modifying the work is outside the purview of the worker. Management defines the work and oversees its performance according to the specifications of the job description.

Management's role in defining, designing, and overseeing the work requires formal meetings for decisions concerning work in 20th century organizations. In these meetings, workers provide information and express opinions, but management makes the decisions. The worker incorporates the decisions into the work. The importance of formal meetings as a means for making decisions indicates the expectations that changes will occur in the work infrequently and only after management carefully deliberates on any proposed changes.

The fourth characteristic of the 20th century transactional relationship is the minimal importance attached to the workers' personal engagement with the organization's mission and values in the context of the transactional relationship. Since the basis of the transaction is the specific work requirements, the mission and values are inconsequential at the individual worker level. The job description defining the specific requirements of the job and the compensation provided by the organization form the basis of the relationship.

Most 20th century healthcare organizations incorporate the mission, vision, and values into the professional standards of the medical staff and nursing. The leadership in these professional groups is responsible for ensuring that the professional standards are met, and in meeting these, the organization as a whole is viewed as fulfilling the mission and vision that it is called to uphold. These professional standards guide the development by management of policies and procedures. The worker, for the most part, does not expect to find a mission and vision as a meaningful aspect of the work or inherent in the work. Workers perform the work as defined by management with expectations of compensation. Management did not expect specific knowledge of the mission beyond a cursory statement in the job description.

The fifth characteristic of the 20th century transactional relationship relates to the positional power of management and negotiations with workers for compensation in exchange for specific labor and level of responsibilities. Workers and management view each other from different sides of the transaction. The transactional relationship puts the emphasis on the documentation that establishes the roles and responsibilities of each side. The personal values of the two remain undefined outside the document, but the very nature of the transaction raises questions on whether the worker and management view each other as partners or adversaries.

The relationship as a transaction depends on the negotiated agreement rather than the engagement of the individuals with each other. When management finds it necessary to make changes and to implement new policies, workers hired to perform tasks in accordance with the plans of management may receive little notice of the changes. Within this context, the workers may find that they cannot align the professed values of management with the actions taken in the new plans or policies.

In considering the five characteristics of the 20th century transactional relationship, the nature of the relations between management and the workers focuses on the role of the worker to provide labor and the role of management as defining, designing, and overseeing the work. The basis for the relationship is the job description that defines the work and the compensation. Given this foundation for the relationship, the worker's contributions to the organization are limited to the work and to the specific expectations of the job requirements. This arrangement strengthens the hierarchical structure within which it flourished by limiting access to information, placing the emphasis of fulfilling specific tasks and job requirements, and management holding the workers accountable for fulfilling their requirements (Goodwin 2015).

In this context, the mission and vision of the organization become background noise to the actual performance of the work. As with any transaction based on the fulfillment of specific requirements, each party expects to monitor compliance with terms of the agreement by the other party. The agreement nature of transactional relationships between workers and management incorporate an element of distrust. When actions by management appear inconsistent with the letter or spirit of the transaction, the compliance aspect becomes the focus of the relationship for the workers. For 20th century healthcare, the transaction of the job description and the monitoring of mutual compliance shaped the essential nature of the relationship between management and the workers.

21st Century Emergent Relationship

In the 21st century, healthcare organizations enter into employment relationships with people; the relationship includes expectations that work will emerge as employees perform activities within the context of the complex system. This emergence or work creation develops from new understandings of the work and new applications of the mission and values of the organization that occur each day. As information systems accelerate the rate of information flow, employees confront situations requiring rapid, independent decision making. In this context, the culture of the organization is much more an understanding of the mission, goals, and values than it is the job description designed by management. Individuals and groups use simple rules that operationalize the mission and values to shape their decisions and activities. Organizational culture emerges within the context of multiple relationships adapting to the common mission and values. Goals and responsibilities emerge as the system adapts to the environment. Functions and roles emerge in response to system needs.

Five possible characteristics for the 21st century emergent relationship under the organization relationship transition are as follows: (1) job description and compensation linked to system goals; (2) mission and values applied to work are the basis for evaluation; (3) frequent decision making at the operational level define the job; (4) mission, vision, and values clearly applied to work; and (5) mission and values consistently expressed in actions by management.

For the first characteristic of the 21st century emergent relationship, the organization and employees consider compensation as based on a broader system perspective than the simple tasks of the 20th century worker. Within the network of the 21st century healthcare organization, each individual is a part of the whole and contributes to the creation of the whole system. Linking the job description and the work and compensation of each individual to the system recognizes the inherent connection to the whole that underlies everyone's work. Though the individual worker may not always recognize this connection due to the work or location, it is incumbent upon management to work to highlight this connection through compensation and support to confirm it in the mind of each employee. Maintaining this system connection is a key management task because of the significance of each individual's role in maintaining the system. Anyone in the system that fails to support the work or communicate effectively reduces the ability of the system as a whole to function due to the interdependencies between functions and services.

In considering the second characteristic of the 21st century emergent relationship, the contrast with the 20th century could not be greater. Whereas the 20th century transactional relationship limited the involvement of workers in the broader perspectives of the organization's mission, vision, and values, the 21st century seeks to promote this involvement by linking work evaluations to these critically important concepts and beliefs. The need for a clear understanding of the application of the mission, vision, and values to the work of each person lies in the nature of the system. If any one individual within the system does not operate with a clear sense of these fundamental understandings, the entire system suffers because of the number of other individuals, functions, and services that each person interacts with on a daily basis.

Management must take the lead in encouraging individuals to recognize the implications of the mission, vision, and values by linking them to the work of the individual and showing the individual the connection to the system as a whole. Building this conception and structure into the evaluation process reinforces for the individual and reminds management of the importance of the people who perform the work and the people who support them that they are inextricably tied together in the web of the organization.

The third possible characteristic of the 21st century emergent relationship points to the need for the people actively involved in performing the work to take a lead in any changes or improvements to the way the work is performed. Frequent informal gatherings and discussions among the employees attended by management take the place of the formal management meetings of the 20th century healthcare organizations. Employees share experiences and ideas about ways to improve the work and ways the mission and values apply to the work. Through their stories and experiences in informal meetings, employees define their jobs and describe the emergence of their understanding of the work and the application of the values and mission of the organization within the context of their specific area. In sharing these insights, employees support the emergence of new ways of working and new applications of the values that other employees can use. This sharing creates the organization as the ideas and experiences ripple from employee to employee. Management attends these gatherings to support and encourage and to promote the sharing as a means for facilitating changes.

For the 21st century healthcare organization, change occurs continuously due to multiple factors in the environment and within the organization. This need to adapt requires frequent informal meetings by staff in the area or in connected areas to work out changes, obtain rapid approval, and move quickly to implement. The meetings are relatively short and clearly focused and involve only the necessary parties. The arrangements are simple, and the responses are quick. Everyone senses the need to address issues quickly in order not to slow down the system response rate. Perhaps the most important part of this process is the belief that small changes made on a frequent basis by the people performing the work ultimately end up in producing meaningful change on a large scale. This system dynamic works for 21st century healthcare organizations.

The fourth characteristic of the 21st century emergent relationship highlights the necessity of clearly expressed and reinforced mission, vision, and values as fundamental to the operation of the entire organization. Due to the fluidity, interconnectivity, and interdependencies that are inherent in the system, the tendency of small changes to permeate the system quickly is ever present. To combat the potential for negative small changes to cause damage to the whole, the mission, vision, and values serve as a decision-making framework to be used by every individual in the system when confronted with a decision. Individuals and groups make countless decisions concerning all aspects of the work throughout the system every day. To ensure consistency in these decisions across the system, the mission and values provide the context for all decisions at all levels of the organization. Referencing the foundational concepts of the mission and values provides a basis for decisions that are more consistent and for responding at the individual level as the system would respond at the system level. This framework is critically important to sustain the efficiency and consistent level of service required for the system.

Though the application of the mission and values seems difficult, practicing this method of addressing issues and making decisions leads to a comfort level over time. Like the simple rules that guide many natural phenomena, 21st century healthcare organizations need to cultivate the ability to apply these principles to different situations to preserve the inherent cohesion of the system. With even small changes, multiple replications can result in significant system changes before anyone realizes that the change is occurring. The mission and values provide a framework for employees to feel confident that they can respond to situations in a way that is consistent across the organization.

For individuals with positional power and individuals who serve as leaders, the fifth characteristic of the 21st century emergent relationship may be the most problematic. Learning to apply the organization's values is difficult and requires a commitment that can be challenging. However, a greater challenge for each individual leader is to act in a way that employees throughout the organization perceive to be consistent with the values of the organization. This is the acid test for employees as they consider their own decisions, actions, and leadership. The model that management exhibits in the incorporation of the values into their personal actions and decisions is a powerful statement to employees throughout the organization. Though it is a high calling, management at all times must demonstrate personal and organizational commitment to the mission and values not just to retain their credibility but also to enable the organization as a complex system to express the same values in all of its operations and interactions with patient-customers. Without this type of commitment by management and anyone exercising leadership, the rest of the organization will chafe at the insistence that everyone follow the values.

Beyond the influence on individual employees that results from leadership's commitment to practicing the values, it also makes a statement to the customers and community within which the organization functions. Clearly stating the values and actively applying the values in the work of the organization in whatever context that may occur produce an awareness that the organization can be trusted in what it says and does. This trust is the result of consistent behavior in following the values.

For the 21st century healthcare organizations, the relationships that exist within the organization and with the customers and communities outside the organization emerge through the interactions that occur every day. As individuals and groups of employees interact together and with people on the outside of the organization, they establish, build, and shape the relationships that actually define the organization. The organization is not a building, and it is not a piece of paper either. It emerges out of the interactions that occur in each encounter, and it comes to life at these points of contact. In looking at the nature of 21st century healthcare as a complex system, the key elements that govern the

20th century transactional relationship	Points (neg)	21st century emergent relationship	Points (pos)
Task-specific job description defines work and compensation		Job description and compensation linked to system goals	
Evaluations focus on specific tasks		Mission and values applied to work as basis for evaluations	
Job and work defined by management		Frequent decision-making at the operational level define job	
Specific application of organization mission and values to the work is not defined		Mission, vision, and values clearly applied to work	
Management modeling of mission and values inconsistent		Mission and values consistently expressed in actions by management	
Total (record on scorecard)		Total (record on scorecard)	

Figure 12.2 Example—Organizational transition relationship characteristics assessment chart.

relationship between employees and management are bound up in the mission, vision, and values. In this way, the 21st century healthcare organization emerges not as a document or as a building but as a living, dynamic entity in which people realize their potential and enable others to realize theirs as they live and adapt to a constantly changing environment (see Figure 12.2).

Chapter 13

Organizational Transition: Leadership—Control to Trust

The third organizational transition is the leadership transition (see Figure 13.1). This transition begins with the 20th century control category as the traditional way in which healthcare organizations viewed the principal role of positional power. The continuum of this transition ends with the 21st century trust category that reflects the new way of viewing the role of leadership in 21st century organizations. To use the leadership transition assessment chart, identify five characteristics in your organization that fit the 20th century control category, and document them in the column. In the 21st century column, identify five characteristics of 21st century leadership trust in your organization that represent changes from the 20th century control characteristics. Using the transition assessment chart, identify the dominant characteristic, the 20th or 21st century, currently in your organization, and assign a 1 in the column for that characteristic. When you have completed the assessment of the five characteristics in each category, total the columns, and document the totals on the transitions scorecard. The sum of the columns based on the comparison of the dominance of the characteristics indicates whether the organization reflects the 20th century model or has progressed to a 21st century healthcare organization structure.

As a reminder from the Introduction of this book, the terms "leader," "leadership," and "position power or positional power" are important in understanding organizational changes between the 20th and 21st centuries in healthcare. The definition for leader in this book is "someone who leads" (Merriam-Webster Online Dictionary) as a simple way of indicating that it may be what someone does (functional) or what someone is. "Position power" and "positional power" in this book refer to "authority and influence bestowed by a position or office on whoever is filling or occupying it" (BusinessDictionary.com). "Manager" and "management" or the specific title (e.g., Chief Executive Officer [CEO]) will refer to "someone who is in charge of a business or department" (Merriam-Webster Online Dictionary) by the position that they hold. "Administrator" is often used to

97

20th century control	Points (neg)	21st century trust	Points (pos)
Total (record on scorecard)		Total (record on scorecard)	

Figure 13.1 Organizational transition leadership characteristics assessment chart.

designate the top management position in a hospital and "administration" is used as a term for the top management of a hospital.

Leadership in 20th century healthcare often referred to individuals holding high positions on the organization chart usually with a title that starts with "C." It did not distinguish between leadership and positional power. The 21st century view of leadership that is emerging offers a very different perspective (Uhl-Bien and McKelvey 2008). Based on ideas associated with relational leadership theory, Uhl-Bien (2006) offers a perspective on leadership that more closely reflects 21st century healthcare's nature as a complex system. Leadership relationships no longer adhere to roles or positions as within the traditional hierarchical structure of healthcare organizations but occur throughout the organization (Uhl-Bien 2006). Social order and action within 21st century healthcare organizations emerge out of the interactive dynamics identified as relational leadership (Uhl-Bien 2006).

In 21st century healthcare, the complex system is the basis for understanding relational leadership and for recognizing the socially constructed roles and relationships of leadership (Uhl-Bien 2006). Leadership is less defined by the title and position and more by the ability and willingness of individuals to respond to changes and exercise leadership in the moment it is needed and where it is needed. Leadership in the future for healthcare organizations emerges as it is needed and shifts from person to person and from place to place to address changes that require responses in real time. There are still defined positions that exercise management roles, but the actual exercise of leadership arises from the interactions occurring within the complex system rather than from a position or a set of prerogatives. Individuals functioning as leaders demonstrate relational transparency and trust as they engage with others (Uhl-Bien and McKelvey 2008).

20th Century Control

Positions high on the organization chart during the 20th century in American healthcare emphasized control as a distinctive aspect of their role in the organization. Working through the hierarchical structure, clear lines of control and reporting created a bureaucracy designed to function efficiently and to provide reports from departments to the positions that exercised control. Five possible characteristics for 20th century control category under the organization leadership transition discussed above are as follows: (1) positional power identified on organizational chart; (2) positional power characterized by control; (3) positional power of control used in pursuit of efficiency; (4) positional power controls access to resources; and (5) positional and professional power restricts leadership by employees. These characteristics provide examples of 20th century control leadership based on positional power and control of resources.

The first characteristic of 20th century control addresses the issue of positional power. Like officer ranks in the military or clerical hierarchy in churches, manufacturing developed hierarchies with specific positions designated as supervisors, managers, administrators, vice presidents, and presidents to exert control over the workers in the organizations. As organization charts became popular, beginning with railroads, which were the most advanced organizations of the early 20th century, the concept of a position on the organization chart representing power became more common. Positions located at the top of the organization chart held the power over positions and departments lower down on the chart.

The chart described graphically the relationships between the positions with power located near the top and the positions and departments that were subordinate further down the chart. The chart used the metaphors "up" and "down" as descriptive of the levels of power and prestige of position on the chart. By going up the chart, people could identify in simple terms the increase in power and prestige for positions higher on the chart. By going down, positions decreased in power and prestige in relation to those at the top. This graphic representation of power and prestige created a powerful image of the dominant role of positions near the top of the chart.

Positional power came into hospitals easily with the administrator overseeing hospital operations and supervisors reporting to the administrator (Rosenberg 1987). Just as in manufacturing, these positions derived their power from the connections with the board that oversaw the operations of the hospital and provided the funding. The organization chart in healthcare followed the models in industry in the display of the positions of power. This structure remains prevalent in most hospitals today as evidenced by the continued use of the traditional hierarchical organization charts to identify positions of power.

The second characteristic of 20th century control relates to positional power characterized by control. Individuals in positions of power in 20th century healthcare organizations expressed their power through their ability to control positions and departments below them on the organization chart. These positions of power exerted control over resources, staff, policies and procedures, and the activities of the departments that reported to them. Exerting positional power to control, manage, and make decisions gave the individuals with positional power significant influence in the organization and over the lives of the workers and middle-level managers. Recognizing when to exert control and how best to exercise it proved challenging, and individuals who held positional power found their credibility questioned when they overreached. Unfortunately, the need to justify the positional power can lead to abuses that cause it to be ineffective.

The third characteristic of 20th century control relates to organizational goals for the distribution of power to positions. As the organization charts identified positions with power, the expectation at the top of the chart and below the positions of power was that the ability to exert control produced desirable results. Individuals in 20th century healthcare organizations with positional power viewed efficiency as the essence of scientific management (Taylor 1911; Rosenberg 1987). The power inherent in certain positions was the basis for managing resources, staff, and the design of work to achieve the highest possible levels of efficiency. Efficiency in early 20th century hospitals took on a variety of meanings from effective management of accounting to centralized control of a diverse workforce. Metaphors of the military, machines, and factories that exemplified efficiency provided models for ways organizations such as hospitals could increase efficiency through proper management of the bureaucracy (Rosenberg 1987).

The fourth characteristic of control relates to resources. In bureaucracies, the ability to obtain and use resources represents the strongest power of control that organizations bestow. Since control of resources in the form of money, staff, equipment, and other assets directly affects the organization's ability to operate, individuals with positional power express their influence in the areas they control by managing the distribution and use of resources. Accountability for the results of the use of resources through reporting up to positions of power further establishes the role of the positions as controlling the work of the organization. By holding subordinate areas accountable for their success in using resources, positional power increases.

The fifth characteristic of control specific to healthcare relates to professional power and the way positional and professional power limit leadership by employees. Just as positions on the organization chart indicate power to allocate resources and direct the staff, professional power of the high-ranking clinical staff accompanies the white coat and the ability to direct the care of patients. Physician control in the 20th century healthcare came from writing orders to direct patient care processes and the use of resources in the care of patients. Physician orders directed the activities of staff from nursing to laboratory and imaging through orders for tests, treatments, and other care processes. Physicians exercise power like individuals with positional power exercise control over resources.

Positional and professional power expressed as control in the 20th century healthcare restricted the leadership opportunities of employees throughout healthcare organizations. In the form of the bureaucracy graphically displayed in the organization chart, healthcare positions located high on the chart control the work and resources of hundreds of staff and millions of dollars. At the same time, the professional power of the physician, though not on the organization chart, controls many of the functions and resources of the staff in the care of patients. The exercise of positional and professional power focused on control of resources, work, and the activities of staff. This control restricted the ability of staff to exercise leadership and limited the ability of individuals with power to accept leadership from the staff. Through their unique history and culture, healthcare organizations retained their structures of bureaucratic and professional power and prestige to the present day with inherent limitations on leadership by the staff.

21st Century Trust

As healthcare organizations define what it means to transition to the 21st century, the nature of leadership shifts from the association with positions of power to the function of leadership regardless of the positions. When this occurs, individuals in positions of power must acknowledge that leadership occurs throughout the organization, and this requires a shift from control to trust. This shift is not because individuals in positions of power want to give up their control. The change represents the reality of healthcare organizations as complex systems. The speed of the changes and the number of decisions made each day exceed the ability of the people in positions of power to respond effectively. Even monitoring activities in a complex system when thousands of contacts and interactions may occur every day overwhelms efforts to exert control except in superficial ways. For organizations to function effectively in this new world of healthcare, leadership must be redefined to provide the type of support that fits this new structure, and the definition of leadership must be broadened to encompass the decisions made by employees at every level (Uhl-Bien and McKelvey 2008).

Five possible characteristics for 21st century trust under the organization leadership transition are as follows: (1) leadership redefined as a capability of anyone willing to take the lead or offer help; (2) leadership exercised by employees throughout an organization based on mission, values, and simple rules; (3) individuals encouraged to exercise leadership in responding to changes or needs; (4) individuals exercising leadership access resources based on simple rules; and (5) positional and professional power positions trust leadership exercised by employees. These characteristics provide examples of the way 21st century trust differs from 20th century control.

The first characteristic of leadership in a culture of trust points to the way in which 21st century healthcare organizations need to think of leadership differently if they are to successfully negotiate the rapid changes and the many challenges that lie ahead. Redefining leadership in a broader sense of anyone at anytime who is willing to help creates an entirely new sense of leadership that can be very powerful in organizations such as hospitals that are functioning as networks. As employees interact with each other and patient-customers, there are numerous situations daily in which an issue arises that needs to be addressed, and someone needs to take the lead in addressing it. If there is an employee who is not in a position of power and wishes to take a leadership role in coordinating the resolution of the issues, then this person is a de facto leader. By broadening the definition of leaders and leadership, healthcare organization in the 21st century will seek to utilize all their resources by empowering employees at all levels to act as leaders when there is an opportunity.

The second characteristic of 21st century trust comes from the increasing complexity of healthcare organizations in which change accelerates, and there is the need to create a structure to support employees as they exercise leadership on a daily basis. Creating a structure based on the mission, values, and simple rules enables employees at the local level to exercise leadership as required to resolve issues. Delays from relaying issues to a central group slow work and dissatisfy patient-customers. Employees in the 21st century need a structure that provides the framework and tools for them to exercise leadership as the need arises. Employees make decisions based on the mission and values of the organization, and simple rules create the parameters of the decisions.

As employees confront different situations each day in which they need to resolve conflicts, they need guidance in shaping their exercise of leadership. The mission of the organization is the premier expression of the reason that the organization exists, and it forms a powerful statement for employees who are seeking to understand their role in the organization. When power positions and others that manage operations talk about the mission and describe how it informs their actions and decisions, employees recognize that the mission is designed to be a dynamic aspect of the work of the organization and that it is to be applied to daily decisions. The mission for the organization creates the priorities that employees can recognize and use to help them choose between two courses of action. It is within the context of these types of decisions that employees struggle to make decisions, and a clear understanding of the priorities improves the efficiency and consistency of the decisions without constantly wasting time by seeking approval. Enabling this type of decision making expresses trust in employees.

Leadership based on organizational values serves the best interest of the organization, the employees, and the customers. Drawing on these values when confronted with an ethical decision or a choice that involves conflicting values, individuals exercising leadership apply the methodology that brings these values into the life of the organizations. When employees see this type of decision making and observe values shaping leadership, it helps them to appreciate the role of values in the life of the organization. This builds trust in the decisions and leadership throughout the organization. It creates an organizational culture of trust.

Simple rules that govern operations function in a similar way, but the application is different. The simple rules for operations provide the guidelines for activities. Simple rules relate to the organic nature of organizations in that they function to guide the frequently occurring processes that replicate and serve as the essential nature of the organization. As employees perform their work and interact with each other, they need to know how each of them will approach work so that they can move efficiently together. With the simple rules for operations, each employee knows what the others will be thinking as they move through their processes and carry out their work. This makes it easier to synchronize work and to recognize when work is not coming together in the best way.

The third characteristic of 21st century culture of trust involves encouragement for employees to exercise leadership. As individuals in positions of power promote the expectations that everyone is capable of leadership and consistently reflects the mission and values of the organization in their activities, employees throughout the organization come to understand that the basis of leadership lies with the fulfillment of the mission and values of the organization. Consistent expression of the mission and values throughout the organization promotes the realization of the mission and establishes support for the values as guiding work.

Of all the responsibilities assigned to power positions, the most problematic to share is the ability to access resources when they are needed. The fourth characteristic of 21st century trust recognizes that this is difficult, but it also recognizes that it is important in assessing the progress of healthcare organizations in preparing for the future. If employees with specified limits have the ability to use resources to solve problems, the ability of the organization to accelerate problem resolutions and to satisfy the needs of patients and customers expands significantly.

The ability to obtain resources is a jealously guarded prerogative, and anyone outside of the positions of power using and accessing resources raises concerns about the potential for loss if employees use the resources inappropriately. These are critical aspects of the problem but surmountable by permitting a limited level of access that can be provided to employees without threatening management. At the same time, employees who are responsible and often use very expensive equipment and supplies can be trusted to use a limited amount of other resources in prescribed ways.

The fifth possible characteristic of 21st century culture of trust involves individuals with positional and professional power recognizing the need for leadership in all areas and trusting employees to lead with appropriate structures when the need arises. Leadership is a function of the interactions between individuals and groups rather than a possession of a person holding a position or practicing a profession. The move from positional power of the 20th century to the new reality of a rapidly changing complex system highlights the role of each employee as a leader in different situations and leadership as a product of the relationships that exist between employees. The speed of the activities of the network and the connectivity of the system in which information flows continuously make it impossible for the positions of power to actively control and manage work as they did before. Their work in this environment is to create relationships of trust with employees built on shared goals and values and consistency in the application of those values.

Employees in this environment are required to make decisions quickly that affect customers and patients. In making these decisions, they express leadership as a part of their work. In working with fellow employees and entities outside

20th century control	Points (neg)	21st century trust	Points (pos)
Positional power identified on the organization chart		Leadership redefined as anyone willing to take the lead or offer help	
Positional power characterized by control		Leadership exercised by employees throughout organization based on mission, values, and simple rules	
Positional power used in pursuit of efficiency		Individuals encouraged to exercise leadership in responding to changes or needs	
Positional power controls access to resources		Individuals exercising leadership access resources based on simple rules	
Positional and professional power restricts leadership by employees		Positional and professional power positions trust leadership exercised by employees	
Total (record on scorecard)		Total (record on scorecard)	

Figure 13.2 Example—Organizational transition leadership characteristics assessment chart.

the organization, they behave as leaders when the need arises by coordinating with other people and arranging responses that resolve the issues. They need guidance to make these decisions and to demonstrate leadership in a way that is consistent with the organization as a whole. They also need to know that they have the support of the organization in making these decisions and to trust that the positions of power will support decisions that are based on the mission, goals, and values of the organization.

It is in creating a new definition of leadership that is based on trust and not on control that the new organization is able to draw on the abilities of all the employees to exercise leadership and make decisions. This new approach meets the need of the system to respond quickly while at the same time maintaining consistency in the responses throughout the system (see Figure 13.2).

Chapter 14

Organizational Transition: Innovation—Centralized to Adaptive

The fourth organizational transition is the innovation transition (see Figure 14.1). This transition begins with the 20th century centralized innovation category with the central power positions as the source of innovation. The continuum of this transition ends with the 21st century adaptive innovation that places the source of innovation in the context of employee interactions with patient-customers and work. Use the innovation transition assessment chart, and identify five characteristics in your organization that fit the 20th century centralized innovation category in which innovation comes from central power positions. In the 21st century adaptive innovation category, healthcare organizations identify characteristics that indicate the transition to adaptive innovation arising from the creativity of employees in the context of their work and interactions with patient-customers. Using the transition assessment chart, the sum of the columns based on the comparison of the characteristics indicates whether the organization reflects the 20th century model or has progressed to 21st century healthcare.

Management in 20th century healthcare organizations like 20th century manufacturing was more focused on the output of labor and not as interested in the ideas of workers. Physicians designed and managed the delivery of care, and the hospital bureaucracy provided the support services. Nurses and other staff took orders in an almost military style (uniforms included) and were rewarded for their promptness and efficiency at carrying out orders. Ideas originated in the upper portion of the organizational chart in the centralized positions of power and focused on expanding services, maintaining financials, and meeting the requirements of regulators. These positions generated ideas and initiatives for change. The locus of control and access to system information were limited and protected, and innovation came from above and went down.

105

20th century centralized innovation	Points (neg)	21st century adaptive innovation	Points (pos)
Total (record on scorecard)		Total (record on scorecard)	

Figure 14.1   Organizational transition innovation characteristics assessment chart.

In the 21st century, innovation becomes a daily event, as information flows more rapidly throughout the organization, and adapting to change becomes a routine part of work. It occurs as individuals respond to changes that require innovation. They use their tacit knowledge or knowledge based on their experience, the practice of their work, and their understanding of the mission and values of the organization to recreate work in response to the new situation they perceive (Nonaka and Takeuchi 1995). Once they conceive of the innovation or idea for recreating work in a new way, they make this idea explicit as they share it with others who are able to recognize and respond to it (Nonaka and Takeuchi 1995).

20th Century Centralized Innovation

The hierarchical structure of 20th century healthcare organizations provides a clear image of the way in which positions relate and information flows. It also provides a meaningful representation of the way innovation occurs. In the 20th century centralized innovation category, the top of the organizational chart and the positions of power form the source of innovation as well as control. These positions possess the information necessary to recognize the need for innovation and define and design the structures of the organization. At this level, all of the areas affected by the innovation can be brought together to assess the way in which innovation may affect the organization as a whole. The top of the organization chart links the bureaucracy and the medical staff in 20th century healthcare organizations and provides the context for incorporating any type of innovation that may affect the physicians.

Five possible characteristics of centralized innovation consistent with 20th century healthcare are as follows: (1) innovation originates from positions of power; (2) innovation recognized only within established channels; (3) innovation spread requires positional power approval; (4) positions of power allocate resources for innovation; and (5) innovations judged by consistency with existing plans.

In the 20th century centralized innovation model, the first characteristic specifically places the origin of innovation in the central positions of power in the development of new services and processes. It is clear that in these organizations, innovation happens as a planned process in which groups come together in formal meetings and develop complex plans for the rollout of innovative services and new products. It is in this environment that the formal structure of control from different parts of the organization comes together with the necessary information and technical support to innovate.

Centralized innovation in 20th century organizations affected not just large-scale innovation but also specific areas of the organization involving only particular departments. The limitations on communications and cooperation between the vertical lines of power and information flow pushed any innovation to the top of the organization to reconcile differences concerning changes between departments. Positions at the top of the organization expected to negotiate any innovation requiring changes in various areas. The employees involved get information from the positions of power about the changes and directions on how they are to work with the innovation.

Recognizing the point of origin of innovation is the focus of the second characteristic of 20th century centralized innovation. Innovation from outside the central leadership is not supported because it arises from a perspective that is foreign to the central group and difficult to integrate into their view of the organization and the way the organization evolves.

Probably the most archaic and emblematic way in which healthcare organization in the 20th century viewed innovation from outside the channels of positional power was the locked suggestion box. The small box placed in a hall somewhere in the organization offered a depository for employees to drop in suggestions on ways to improve the organizations. The few suggestions placed in the box often sits there for a long time, and it may even happen that the key to the suggestion box gets lost. It really does not matter because the source of innovation is at the top of the organization and not in the employees.

Innovation that comes from outside the positions of power appears as disruptive rather than helpful. It tends to be based on more specific situations familiar to employees and less on the global view of the top positions. For top positions to incorporate this type of innovation into the larger picture of the organization requires different approaches and challenges the existing processes of innovation that are built into the system. This type of innovation like the suggestion box represents a specific problem that needs to be addressed at the employee level rather than an innovation that can take the organization in a new direction. Due to the difficulty of working with employees on innovation, avoidance occurs more often than embracing the insight and change they bring to the organization.

The third characteristic of 20th century centralized innovation deals with the spread of innovation and its control by positions of power. The ability of innovation to move through an organization and to propagate in different areas quickly offers an indication of the speed by which the organization is able to adapt to its environment and to internal dynamics. For the 20th century healthcare organizations, slow innovation was preferred to maintain the stability of the organization. There was little sense that rapid change was needed or desirable, and power positions maintained control on the development of innovation and its spread from one area to another.

In managing the movement of new ideas and practices through the organization and restraining change, positional power maintains the façade of the organization as a solid and stable institution that already incorporates the best care and services. The introduction of new ideas and new ways of delivering care is managed to maintain this image of stability because the community and the leadership of the organization want to view the local hospital as a stable and predictable resource capable of meeting the community's needs at all times. Any new equipment or way of practicing medicine is presented, debated, packaged, and announced in a way designed to show that it fits with what currently exists but with small improvements that everyone understands.

Innovation in 20th century healthcare organizations required time to hold formal meetings, to debate the pros and cons, and to deliberate on the implications of change. In the fourth characteristic of 20th century centralized innovation, the time and information resources to innovate belong to the positions of power rather than the individuals at the point of care. Nurses, technicians, and therapists busily delivering care do not have the time to move their ideas forward or to research and evaluate the potential benefits of changes that they may want to make in the way they work or the delivery of care.

The layers of the bureaucracy in 20th century healthcare organizations work very well in filtering out ideas that do not fit the current model of care. For an employee with an idea, finding someone with the interest and ability to move that idea up the hierarchy is difficult. It requires time just to discuss the idea with local management in the department. Time is often the most valuable commodity in a busy department because of the needs of patients. Employees who may want to advance an idea find it difficult to free themselves to move it forward.

The fifth characteristic of 20th century centralized innovation focuses on the nature of the 20th century healthcare organization as understanding the future to be like the past. Innovation that appears in the organization spontaneously or that is introduced into the organization from the outside must meet the initial test of consistency with the past before it moves forward. This critical aspect of the nature of innovation as it exists within this model builds on the understanding of healthcare as an industry that progresses along a set path.

The traditions and practices built into the hospital as an institution provide stability and structure designed to meet the needs of the physicians and the administration for control and management. Deviating from the existing processes and introducing disruptive changes create new workflows and new demands on the system that may threaten the stability of the status quo. Management and physician leaders work within a complex environment of relationships that have basic understandings on how the organization works and how they relate to each other. Introducing changes that affect these relationships or that change processes or the allocation of resources requires negotiations and new understandings. All of this takes time and may even lead to breakdowns. Maintaining the status quo and the stability of the organization is important in order not to disrupt the ability of the hospital to function. The value of this stability outweighs the perceived benefits of enabling innovation.

For the 20th century healthcare organization, innovation is problematic, and the management of it to ensure that it does not interfere with work and the structure of the organization is a priority for the top positions. Innovation in and of itself is not viewed as an essential value to the future of the organization because the future of the organization is perceived to be like the past. Maintaining the stability of the work processes and ensuring the continuance of the general understandings that support the existing relationships are considered much more valuable than innovation.

Positional power in the 20th century hospital works to build and to strengthen relationships within the hospital and the community that facilitate the work of the organization. Positional power carefully manages innovation to prevent it from spreading spontaneously and disrupting the existing processes. When positional power determines the need for innovation, it carefully reviews all aspects of the new process or equipment and tries to anticipate what existing structures and relationships will be affected and how to mitigate any disruptions that may occur. Packaging the change to fit within the current structure maintains the image of stability.

21st Century Adaptive Innovation

Innovation is a hallmark of the future of healthcare, and its role in the organizations and processes are critically important for survival. In the 21st century adaptive innovation, it is important to recognize that innovation flows out of the nature of the organization and interaction of the organization with the environment. It is not innovation for the sake of innovation but rather an adaptive response to a constantly changing environment and the internal dynamics that this change produces within the organization.

Embracing innovation and encouraging it help the organization to discover the best fit with the environment. The source of the innovation is unimportant. The key is being able to recognize that an innovation or idea has potential and to opens channels for it to move through the organization. The ability of the organization to absorb innovation becomes critically important as the sources of innovation spread throughout the organization, and the number of innovations grow. Leadership in the 21st century finds an important new role in promoting and supporting innovation in healthcare organizations.

Five possible characteristics for 21st century adaptive innovation under the organization innovation transition are as follows: (1) innovation emerges where work is performed; (2) innovation supported wherever it occurs; (3) innovation is shared spontaneously, and spread is encouraged throughout the organization;

(4) process set up to make resources for innovation readily available; and (5) innovation judged by success in meeting mission and vision.

The first characteristic of 21st century adaptive innovation focuses on the sources of new ideas and new ways of working. The interface between organizations and the environment offers fertile ground for new ideas because there is flux and potential for a space between the two in which there is room for innovation. As individuals perform their work and as they interact with others in the organization and outside, the cross-pollination that occurs as they try to blend their work and their views of work produces opportunities for new insights that may lead to new ways of performing work.

The most important aspect of this source of innovation is the view that the individuals and groups actively involved in work are the most likely sources of new ways to perform work. In order to promote this perspective, the people involved in work must be encouraged to see their roles as change agents. They must recognize that improving the way they work and the work they perform is as important as work itself. Encouraging and supporting this perspective are important aspects of leadership.

In the 20th century healthcare organization, innovation appears within the context of the hierarchy of command and control. The design of the organization works to reduce the potential for innovation occurring outside of the hierarchy and carefully manages it whenever it appears to ensure that it does not disrupt the stability and structure of the organizations. In a second characteristic of 21st century adaptive innovation, new ideas and new approaches happen frequently throughout the organization. Innovation becomes part of the daily work and activities of employees throughout the system.

In the course of work each day, people at the frontlines of the interface between the organization and its environment, its patient-customers, encounter new situations and new questions that need to be addressed. As they search for ways to respond, they innovate. They come up with new ways of approaching these situations, and some work, and some do not. Regardless of the outcome, it is imperative that these employees as individuals and in groups feel empowered to develop new ideas because they change the organization through their innovations. They are literally creating the organization each day through their interactions, and innovations that provide new answers are part of that process.

Supporting this innovation is an important leadership function. This support may be through the immediate openness of the culture at the point of care to consider new approaches. The support may be a supervisor, manager, or director that encourages employees to look for new ways to perform work. It may be in the words of the Chief Executive Officer (CEO) who appeals to employees to think creatively and to go the extra distance to develop innovative approaches. The support for innovation throughout the organization is literally support for the future of the organization as innovation is the basis for survival in that future.

When innovation occurs, it is more likely to die at conception than to be spread due to the barriers to innovation inherent in organizations. As the third characteristic of 21st century adaptive innovation, the focus is on sharing new ideas and encouraging the adoption of new approaches throughout the organization. Employees are encouraged to innovate and then to share their innovation with others because it is through the grassroots efforts of employees talking with each other and sharing new ways of doing work that innovation permeates the organization.

Encouraging the spread of innovation requires a conscious effort to design the organizational structure, the facilities, and the culture to welcome innovation and to promote its spread spontaneously. Creating connections between departments and functions that may be outside of their normal work processes brings together people from different areas who may not often interact to encourage the sharing of ideas that may be very different. The facilities designed with open spaces encourage cross-pollination between work areas. Finally, the culture promotes innovation through the recognition of it as it appears.

New ideas develop in a moment of inspiration and in the midst of work. An employee encounters a situation and recognizes a potentially new way of doing work that may be more efficient, provide better service, or achieve better outcomes. The fourth characteristic of 21st century adaptive innovation identifies the need for resources to move ideas forward and for the organization to recognize that this is worth the investment. It is difficult within complex organizations to allocate resources quickly and easily because of the layers set up to protect resources. Positions of power control the access and use of resources. Certain services have access to resources. Outside of these channels, however, access to resources may be limited, and it may be difficult for individuals or groups to obtain resources to try new ideas or to conduct additional research on the potential. Simply the process for trying to access resources dooms many innovations before they mature.

The process for making resources available to move ideas from conception to future implementation needs to be built into the system by opening the access and promoting the use of resources for innovation. This requires a conscious decision by management to set up an innovation processing function within the organization that makes resources and support readily available. In the 21st century healthcare organization, the importance of innovation to the future and to the ability of the organization to respond quickly and effectively to changes in the environment justifies investment in ideas that may help to create that future. This view of innovation and the use of resources provide the incentive for the development of processes that support innovation.

Innovation is problematic within organizations because it is different from what is and what may be expected. By its very nature, it creates disruption in the normal flow of work by suggesting that a better way exists. In addressing the judgment of innovation, the fifth characteristic of 21st century adaptive innovation speaks to the evaluative processes that the organization uses to support or suppress innovation and the implementation of new ideas. As new ideas appear, and individuals and groups promote their acceptance and work to incorporate them into the organization, evaluation is a necessary part of the process.

The judgment of new ideas must be rooted in the mission, vision, and values that are the foundation for the organization as a whole. Innovation consistent with the mission, vision, and values of the organization moves forward. New ideas that are inconsistent with the mission, vision, and values are similarly judged and found to be inconsistent and are relegated to a lesser status in which they become part of the processes of innovation but not promoted for acceptance within the organization.

Judgment of innovation as consistent with the mission, vision, and values helps to filter out ideas so that time and the resources of the organization can be focused on ideas that are clearly consistent with the basic nature of the organization and with its ways of doing business and its views of the future. It is important that this evaluation focuses on these foundational filters rather than the consistency of innovation with the current plans for the organization or current operational priorities. It is very likely that innovation by its very nature will not be consistent with what is currently happening at the time the innovation appears. Using current status as the evaluative key severely limits innovation and restricts the ability of the organization to recognize potentially useful ideas.

In the 21st century healthcare organization, innovation arises naturally out of the dynamic environment within which the organization functions. It is adaptive innovation because it is born of the need for a new approach that emerges from the interface of the changing environment and the organization's response to the changes. The challenge for the 21st century healthcare organization is accommodating this naturally occurring response and harnessing the energy and creative drive that it embodies.

The most important aspect of the incorporation of adaptive innovation into healthcare organizations is the recognition that innovation arises out of work and not only as a function of positional power. This is a critical aspect because without the understanding that new ideas develop wherever work is performed, the organization will not be able to recognize innovation when it occurs and will not be able to absorb and benefit from it. Creating the channels to guide new ideas emerging from work is the structural imperative that 21st century organizations must address to manage this creative impulse.

Recognizing and channeling innovation from all points in the organization to all other places where it can be useful is an organizational challenge. The spread of innovation requires the organization to find ways to promote communication between various areas. This means the creation of new spaces for meetings and new opportunities for individuals and groups to interact. It also means making resources available to encourage efforts to trial innovation with the expectations that these trials may not work. The willingness to make it easy for resources to be applied to innovative ideas supports innovation itself and promotes the spread of new ideas. It also provides the organization with the means for testing and refining new ideas that are promising.

20th century centralized innovation	Points (neg)	21st century adaptive innovation	Points (pos)
Innovation originates from positions of power		Innovation emerges where work is performed	
Innovation recognized only within established channels		Innovation supported wherever it occurs	
Innovation spread requires positional power approval		Innovation is shared spontaneously and spread is encouraged throughout organization	
Resources for innovation allocated by power positions		Process set up to make resources for innovation readily available	
Innovations are judged by consistency with existing plans		Innovation judged by success in meeting mission and vision	
Total (record on scorecard)		Total (record on scorecard)	

Figure 14.2   Example—Organizational transition innovation characteristics assessment chart.

Finally, the judgment of innovation must move from the test of consistency with the status quo to the test of fulfilling the mission, vision, and values of the organization. Innovation by definition will be inconsistent with the status quo and difficult for the existing organization to absorb. Using the mission as the basis for evaluating new ideas and for judging the success of innovation provides the flexibility and foundation for innovation to move beyond the existing reality and to open the way to a new approach that takes the organization to a higher level (see Figure 14.2).

Chapter 15

Process Transition: Production Method—Craftsman to Multidisciplinary Teams

The first process transition is the production method transition (see Figure 15.1). This transition begins with the 20th century craftsman category with the role of the licensed practitioner, most often a physician, defined as an independent craftsman. The continuum of this transition ends with the 21st century multidisciplinary team in which patient care is a team responsibility, and the practitioner is a member of the team. Within 20th century craftsman production, healthcare organizations identify the characteristics in which practitioners continue to provide care as craftsmen. In the 21st century multidisciplinary team category, healthcare organizations identify characteristics that indicate the transition to teams of professionals delivering care. Using the production method transition assessment chart, the sum of the columns based on the comparison of the characteristics indicates whether the organization reflects the 20th century or has progressed to 21st century healthcare.

The production method process transitions from 20th to 21st century healthcare represent significant changes in the processes that produce healthcare. These processes involve the production of healthcare as it moves from the independent craftsman practitioner in the small community to the multidisciplinary team that is able to bring all the knowledge and expertise of healthcare to bear in accomplishing the goals of the patient. American healthcare in the 18th and much of the 19th century consisted of people in small towns sharing knowledge and experience to benefit each other. In this craftsman model of healthcare, individuals with knowledge or experience delivered care to other people in the same way that a carpenter prepared a chair for a customer. The quality and efficacy of healthcare were directly related to the ability of the individual physician or town herbalist. If the outcomes were good more often than not, then the people would

115

20th century craftsman production	Points (neg)	21st century multidisciplinary team	Points (pos)
Total (record on scorecard)		Total (record on scorecard)	

Figure 15.1 Process transition production method characteristics assessment chart.

seek out the service of the local care provider the same way they would any other craftsman.

Due to the efforts of the American Medical Association and the specialization of physicians around new technology and surgery, the role of the physician as a professional developed. This role eclipsed the efforts of others to participate in the care of patients except in subservience to the physicians. This process was institutionalized through licensure to prescribe and write orders and membership in the medical staff of local hospitals. This 20th century model places all of the responsibility for the processes of care on the physician as well as all the prerogatives of care (Starr 1982).

With the expansion of information systems as well as the rapid growth of healthcare research and knowledge, 21st century healthcare expanded into many areas, and new fields of specialization developed. The physician is no longer able to comprehend all that is known or needs to be known to care for patients. As physicians have become employees of health systems, and as new specialties brought nonphysicians into the care process, multidisciplinary teams developed. Groups of care providers from various disciplines share processes and measure outcomes. Group decisions made on care delivery and the ability to modify care in response to changes without the direct involvement of the physician represent moves on the continuum toward a broader care team approach.

20th Century Craftsman Production

Craftsman production places the emphasis on the art of medicine rather than the science when it is applied to the licensed practitioner and particularly the physician. Healthcare organizations and their patients in the 20th century viewed physicians as a scientist in terms of training and knowledge but as an artist in terms of the application of that knowledge to the individual patient. Patients expected the physician as a practitioner of the art of medicine to formulate a unique understanding and plan of care for them in the same way that an artist creates a unique painting for a client. As a scientist, patients expected the physician to be a knowledgeable and skilled practitioner capable of bringing the latest medical developments to the bedside.

Five possible characteristics that portray the nature of the craftsman as the method of production in healthcare are as follows: (1) practitioners work alone;

(2) practitioners set the goals for their patients; (3) practitioners resist peer review, quality metrics, and standardization; (4) practitioners control all aspects of care; and (5) practitioners resist incorporating other disciplines into the care process.

Practitioners who operate as a craftsman bring the perspective of the artist and the scientist to the care of patients and work alone as described in the first characteristic. Following graduation from medical school and completion of a residency, the 20th century physician obtains a license, joins the local hospital medical staff, and begins to practice the art of medicine in a community. In the past, the physician set up an office as an independent practitioner, but many physicians who retain the craftsman view today are part of large practices. Their view of their work as a craftsman who works alone in their care of their patients and their view of their work as unique shape their practice. It is in this aspect rather than the employment relationship or the size of the practice that sustains the 20th century concept of the craftsman practitioner.

The second characteristic of 20th century craftsman production recognizes that the craftsman practitioners set the goals to their patients. This view of the delivery of care reflects the role of physicians in the past in which they delivered all the care to the patient. The concept of setting goals for their patients was a natural outgrowth of the way they practiced, their licensure, and their view of their work as art customized for every patient. This method of delivering care continues to be reflected in the attitude of patients. Many patients view their physicians as the only ones who understand their needs and can deliver care to them. They do not question physicians, and they are compliant with whatever the physicians order or recommend.

Like any local craftsman, the physician learns about the individual patients and their families and delivers care to meet the needs of the patients. Knowledge of the intimate personal details of patients and their family dynamics places physicians in a position in which trust is a fundamental part of the practice of medicine. This creates a unique bond between the physicians and patients and leads to a very powerful role that the physician plays in the local hospital and the community. Patients trust their physician, and the relationship is equated with that of the priest or the minister.

The strength of the relationships that physicians have with their patients shapes the role of the physician in the 20th century healthcare system. When the patient is sick, they trust their physician to recommend the care they need and to deliver it whether in the office, home, or at the local hospital. The physicians who operate this way expect the hospital to deliver care as the physicians require because the physicians are designing the care to meet the needs of their patients. They expect that their directions for the care of their patients are carried out by the hospital staff because they are responsible for all aspects of the care of their patients.

Once a physician is licensed to practice in a state and becomes a member of the local hospital medical staff, the measure of the quality delivered by the physician in the 20th century is essential to the judgment of the physician delivering the care. Based on this third characteristic of 20th century craftsman production, the physician with training, experience, a license to practice, and approval to use the services of the local hospital independently evaluates the care that is delivered to patients. The satisfaction of the patients in the care delivered and their willingness to continue seeking care from the physician become the measures of the quality of the care just as the finished product is the measure of the quality of any craftsman. Practitioners who view themselves from the craftsman perspective find the application of peer review, quality metrics, and other measures of quality to be an intrusion into their views of the art and science of medicine. Attempts by hospitals to standardize care particularly offend craftsman practitioners who view their work as specifically designed for each patient and not routine or what an agency thinks should happen.

The independent physician's license comes under the state statutes that empower the state medical board to review applications for licensure and to grant licenses after verifying credentials. At the local hospital, the medical staff reviews the credentials of the physicians applying for appointment to the medical staff and votes to approve the application for appointment. After passing these initial reviews by the state and hospital medical staff, they view the physician as capable of delivering good care to patients. It is only in rare cases with clear evidence of malpractice that the state medical board or even the local hospital would consider taking action against a practitioner that has the appropriate credentials. Hospitals and the state assume that the physician delivers good quality of care based on these credentials unless there is an obvious dereliction of duty.

The fourth characteristic of 20th century craftsman production rests on the expectation that physicians will control all aspects of their patients' care. Patients expect that the physicians will provide all the care that they need or will refer them to specialists. In fulfilling this expectation, physicians generate and write all orders, document their assessments about the patient, and determine the care of the patient at the local hospital. The nursing staff recognizes the dominant role of the physicians in the care process and follows the orders explicitly.

As responsible for ordering all of the care that their patients receive, the physicians become the designers of the care process. The hospital designs the basic structure for the admission process and orders, but physicians generate the orders that actually establish the processes of care, the treatment of the patient, and directions for the staff. The essential documentation is the physicians' documentation, and the conclusions that matter are the conclusions expressed by the physicians. This method of delivering care essentially requires that the hospital adapt to the individual preferences and requests of the physicians regardless of how these differ between physicians.

Since the care of their patients is the responsibility of the physicians, and physicians design all of the care delivered to the patient, craftsman physicians use other disciplines, particularly nonspecialists, much less frequently. This fifth characteristic of 20th century craftsman production recognizes the amazingly unique role of physicians in America. All aspects of the care of the patient are contingent on the physician's approval from the medications the patients receive to the patient's ability to walk around to even the patient's ability to leave the hospital, and the staff of the hospital are required to carry out the physician's orders. The use of other disciplines is contingent on the physicians who admitted the patient ordering the consultations or permitting other professionals to work with the patient. For the craftsman practitioner, the involvement of other professions may be viewed as intrusive and not helpful due to their unique approach to the care of their patients.

21st Century Multidisciplinary Team Production

As healthcare passes through industrialization and moves into the 21st century, the independent physician in a solo practice is a rarity rather than a rule. Following major shifts in healthcare regulations, insurance requirements, technological advances, and patient demands, physicians in the new era often work in large practices or as employees in hospitals or health systems.

Five possible characteristics for the 21st century multidisciplinary team under the process production method are as follows: (1) practitioners are part of a multidisciplinary team; (2) care based on patient goals; (3) practitioner quality an element of team quality; (4) team develops plan of care, and practitioner participates in team decisions; and (5) team develops consensus care plan that includes all disciplines.

The first characteristic of the 21st century multidisciplinary team production places the emphasis on the practitioners, particularly physicians, as members of multidisciplinary teams whether in large group practices or in health systems. Included in the group may be a variety of disciplines with well-defined roles in delivering the care to patients. Disciplines represented in the group often possess greater knowledge in specific areas than the individual practitioners or other professions. Often, advance-practice nurses and physician assistants are part of the group and may deliver the majority of the care under the supervision of the physicians who attend to seriously ill or complex patients. Other disciplines that specialize in nutrition or particular diagnoses such as diabetes provide patient education and training when ordered by a physician to help the patient manage their condition more effectively.

As a member of a group or team, physicians work with many disciplines contributing to the care of the patients. The teamwork represents a significant change from the 20th century and broadens the scope of care and the ability to access more resources efficiently. Patients benefit as more providers with different skills participate in the care process. In addition, the team brings a wider array of knowledge and experience to the care process than physicians possess on their own. The team arrangement enables the physicians to focus on the particularly complex aspects of care that their training qualifies them to address.

Being a part of a group that is delivering care places an emphasis on the way everyone uses the processes of care. It is no longer simply one person trying to get things done. Now, coordination of care becomes an important issue, and communication between members of the group is a valuable skill. The need to communicate and to be mindful of others on the team represent a change in the way care is delivered and leads to processes that are suitable for multiple disciplines rather than just one.

The second possible characteristic of the 21st century multidisciplinary team involves the importance of the patient's goals. As patients assume more of the costs of care, they desire a stronger voice in setting the goals of their care. Patients would like to know more about their conditions. The outcomes of care matter to them. Patients want to pay for what they consider valuable or worth the payment. In the team approach, each discipline engaged with the patient strives to identify what they should work to accomplish, and the patient provides the insight that guides them. Operating as a team increases the attention directed to the patient's desires because this helps to create a coordination point for the team and a way to evaluate the quality of care based on the patient-customers' view of what was provided.

For the physicians, the focus on patient goals represents a change in perspective from the 20th century healthcare in which the physician defined the care and the goals of care. Patients bring more information to the process of care and participate more in decisions about their care. Other disciplines participating in the patient's care may have complementary but different goals. Physicians engage with patients more in this new environment to clearly define what the care is to accomplish. This partnership with the patient helps to prevent patient dissatisfaction with the care process results and helps the physician to focus the limited resources on the particular concerns expressed by the patient.

Industrialization made quality an important part of healthcare, and in the third characteristic of the 21st century multidisciplinary team, the quality of care has broadened to include all aspects of the care delivered by the team. It is no longer simply a function of the practitioner's efforts, although this is still a major portion, but is a function of the team's effort to care for the patient. By making the quality of the care a team concern, the care process is viewed in its entirety, and all the members of the team become contributors to the quality.

With quality as a function of the team, the interactions between the patient and the members of the team and the appropriateness, timeliness, and effectiveness of the care all become a part of the evaluation of the care. In the past, physicians defined the quality of care. Any questions of quality became personal questions between the patient and the physician because the physician managed all the care. Multidisciplinary teams focus on the processes of care and use the insights of the members, including the physician and the patients, to improve the care.

Responsibility for the care and the outcomes of care belong to the team in this fourth characteristic of the 21st century multidisciplinary team. Due to the involvement of multiple disciplines, no single individual is responsible for all the decisions. The physician is ultimately the leader in making decisions about the care of the patient, but the team works together to develop the plan of care and to work with the patient in deciding on the goals of care.

Multidisciplinary team members identify many factors about the care process that an individual physician could miss. Discussions concerning the patient's condition, situation, and prospects help everyone on the team to think creatively about ways to meet the patient's needs that are effective and recognize the costs to the patient. Even disagreements about the care help to bring important aspects to the attention of the team. It is in these discussions that new insights are most likely to appear.

In the fifth and final characteristic of the 21st century multidisciplinary team production, the physician's role within the team becomes clearer. The team is responsible for the care of the patient, and the physician has a major role in developing the care plan but ultimately supports the decision of the team. This is significantly different from the 20th century where the physician worked and made decisions alone and took full responsibility. In the 21st century, the team is accountable for the care of the patient, and the physician is part of that team. Placing the responsibility for care on the team characterizes the contrast between the 20th and 21st century approach to patient care.

In reality, this emphasis on the team as the care delivery system recognizes what was true but unacknowledged in the past. The physician's dominance of the actual delivery of healthcare diminished throughout the 20th century even as social deference and the process of care created the illusion of total control. The complexity of healthcare and the multiple disciplines with depths of knowledge beyond the grasp on any individual worked together to come up with the plan of care and to carry out the plan. Acknowledging this reality and designing systems and processes based on this approach represent a major improvement and movement on the continuum toward 21st century healthcare.

Pulling back the curtain to reveal the complexity and breadth of healthcare's multidisciplinary reality represents the endpoint of the production method continuum. Recognizing the continuing major role of the physician but placing it within the context of the multidisciplinary team creates a more efficient and more effective delivery system and a more creative approach to healthcare. This opens up the team dynamic so that each profession contributes, and no discipline overshadows another in the care of the patient. At the same time, the patient's role in setting the goals of care becomes clearer as the focus on the physician diminishes. Within the team, each profession plays a role and takes responsibility for contributing to the fulfillment of the patient's goals.

The multidisciplinary healthcare team of the 21st century takes as its starting point the patient's goals. This becomes the focus as each discipline discusses the care with the patient and with each other, and out of the conversation, the plan and the goals of the plan emerge. By reducing the focus on an individual or a particular discipline, the team is able to redirect the attention of all of the

20th century craftsman production	Points (neg)	21st century multidisciplinary team	Points (pos)
Practitioners work alone		Practitioners part of multidisciplinary team	
Practitioners set goals for patients		Care based on patient goals	
Practitioner resists peer review, quality metrics, standardization		Practitioner quality an element of team quality	
Practitioner controls all aspects of care		Team develops plan of care and practitioners participate in team decisions	
Practitioner resists incorporating other disciplines in care process		Team develops consensus care plan that includes all disciplines	
Total (record on scorecard)		Total (record on scorecard)	

Figure 15.2   Example—Process transition production method characteristics assessment chart.

members on the patient. This focus on the patient enables the team to blend their views, skills, and goals into a common purpose that serves the patient.

The quality of care is a team product rather than the results of one person's efforts, and the team is responsible for developing the plan of care and partnering with the patient to carry it out. The team of professionals brings their various skills and talents to the task of understanding the needs and desires of the patient and building a plan to achieve the goals of the patient. They hold each other accountable for the quality of their work and the integrity of their commitment to the patient. The team forms around the patient through this unique blending of personal and professional contributions and produces the high-quality healthcare that is the vision of the 21st century (see Figure 15.2).

Chapter 16

Process Transition: Delivery System—Hospital to Continuum of Care

The second process transition is the delivery system transition (see Figure 16.1). This transition begins with the 20th century hospital category as the healthcare delivery method that dominated the 20th century. The continuum of this transition ends with the 21st century continuum of care that reflects the diversity of care options proliferating in the 21st century. Within the 20th century hospital category, healthcare organizations identify the characteristics in which their delivery system continues to be hospital based. In the 21st century continuum of care category, the healthcare organizations identify the characteristics that indicate that the delivery system has expanded outside the hospital to encompass a broad range of services and delivery systems. Using the transition assessment chart, the sum of the columns based on the comparison of the characteristics indicates whether the organization reflects the 20th century model or has progressed to a 21st century healthcare organization structure.

A hallmark of 20th century healthcare was the impressive but isolated hospital that served as the healthcare factory of the community. All the resources to deliver the latest healthcare services were in the hospital along with the specialists. In the community, the local physicians were on the medical staff of the hospital and admitted and cared for their patients in that hospital. It was an independent and a cherished symbol of community pride. Services in hospitals were developed and delivered without reference to a continuum of care since most patients went home to care provided by family or private duty nursing. Transfers of patients were managed as individual transactions.

In the 21st century, the hospital is rapidly becoming only one of a number of stops on the continuum of care that begins with primary and preventive care and continues through outpatient and inpatient acute care to a wide variety of post-acute care in facilities or in the home. Care delivery along a

123

20th century hospital	Points (neg)	21st century continuum of care	Points (pos)
Total (record on scorecard)		Total (record on scorecard)	

Figure 16.1 Process transition delivery system characteristics assessment chart.

continuum is still in the developmental stages but is rapidly developing in response to financial and societal pressures. Service delivery is a seamless continuum of care moving through levels of acuity based on patient need with movement of patients facilitated with shared monitoring and measurement of system performance. Agencies share outcomes and payments along the continuum. The delivery system transition assesses the progress in the development of the continuum of care.

20th Century Hospital Delivery System

The aspect of the 20th century healthcare delivery system that points to the reality of the lack of a system is the isolation that characterized the physician and the hospital. Beginning with the physician as the center of the delivery system of healthcare in the 20th century, the hospital emerged as the focal point of technology and support. These two images epitomize American 20th century healthcare as it functioned during the century.

Five possible characteristics for the 20th century hospital category under the process delivery system transition are as follows: (1) patients view hospital as the place for care; (2) no clear picture of the agencies or processes of care in the continuum; (3) care coordination only inside hospital; (4) independent agencies deliver services without reference to other providers; and (5) hospital has limited communication with other care providers.

Like a 19th century factory and with similar architecture, the hospital rises up to take its place in the community's skyline and serves as a beacon for anyone with an injury or illness that needs the benefits of science to protect them or to restore their health. Its role as the center of 20th century healthcare is the first characteristic of the 20th century delivery system. It has the professionals and specialists with the greatest knowledge and experience. It has the latest technology that research and manufacturing can deliver to ensure that any illness or injury can be treated and fixed. It has the facilities to provide for the comfort and care of patients 24/7. In short, the hospital is the quintessential healthcare production facility of the 20th century and the iconic symbol of all humanities yearning for freedom from injury, illness, and death.

In communities across America, the hospital is not only a symbol of healing and hope but also a symbol of the community. The modern hospital in a community becomes a key element for the Chamber of Commerce and local industry to point to as a testimony to the quality of life that the community has to offer. More than any other aspect of community life, the modern hospital shines as a beacon on a hill welcoming newcomers to a place where life is good and where they will be taken care of. This image resonates throughout the American health-care experience of the 20th century.

For residents in the community, the hospital has been a part of their life and healthcare since birth. Born in the hospital, treated in its emergency room, and visiting the elderly dying in its intensive care units, people see the hospital as the place that provides healthcare at all stages of life. This connection is born not only from experience but also from the guidance of the physicians on the medical staff of the hospital who refer their patients to the hospital for testing, operations, and medical care. People in the community think of the hospital as the place to go to receive care, and this is built into the rhythm of life in the community. Any changes to service or facilities may be a serious issue that affects local elections and creates controversy at town meetings. The hospital symbolizes healthcare in 20th century America.

Apart from the hospital, the healthcare system of the local community is difficult to recognize and has no easily identifiable image. The second characteristic of the 20th century delivery system points to the lack of connection between healthcare providers and services. The care processes of the local hospital are contained within the local hospital. The hospital, itself, is a self-contained entity that delivers care and then returns the patient to the community with little real regard for what happens after they leave the healthcare production facility. The medical record in the local hospital is a hardcopy document or is minimally electronic and is inaccessible outside of the hospital. It documents the care of the patient in the hospital but provides little information on the plan for care after the patient leaves the hospital. In terms of care of the patient outside the hospital, the patient typically begins in the physician's office if not in the hospital emergency department and ends with a return to the physician's office. The focus is on the office of the independent practitioner as the point in the community that holds the pieces together and refers patients to various places across the community to access care. There is no clear sense that healthcare services outside of the hospital are connected or that they represent in any sense a connected system of care. They provide services as independent agencies, and the only unifying element is the physician who orders the services or refers the patients.

Most striking in the 20th century model of healthcare is the dominance of the hospital as the context within which healthcare is not delivered in a coordinated fashion. Outside of the hospital, the various healthcare vendors deliver services as independent businesses. Within the hospital, as this third possible characteristic of 20th century delivery system highlights, nurses, case managers, and others follow the orders of the physician and recognize the services as part of the delivery system within the hospital. These disciplines provide care as ordered by the doctor and document the care they deliver. Physicians and nurses choreograph in real time all the pieces of the care process and create a system of care. This is the only point in the healthcare system in which this is the case.

The fourth possible characteristic of the 20th century hospital delivery system highlights the difference between the care in the hospital and the multiple agencies outside the hospitals that deliver care as independent contractors rather than a coordinated system of care. Many pharmacies in the town provide medications and a variety of other goods and services, but they do not work together. They compete for patients. The local nursing homes provide care in the community, but they function as a place to stay for the elderly as they go back and forth to the hospital rather than as a dynamic part of a continuum of care. Home health services compete for business as do durable medical equipment and other specialties and services scattered throughout the community. The referring physician is the common reference point.

In the fifth characteristic of the 20th century hospital delivery system, the hospital is the most visible symbol of healthcare in the community, but its role does not include coordination of the other providers of care in the community. The hospital occupies its unique place in the community as the source of care, but it remains isolated within its own processes of care. Within the hospital, the disciplines delivering care document the care they deliver to inform the physician and for billing but not to inform other agencies or service providers outside the hospital.

The hospital serves as a place that refers patients out for services and as a source of patients for other agencies, but the hospital does not design and manage a system of care in the community. There is no financial incentive to take on the role of coordinating community services except that it assists in the discharge of patients. For patients needing nursing home care following a stay in the hospital, the relationship between the nursing home and the hospital can be important in making sure that beds are readily available for patients when they are ready to leave the hospital. Working as independent service providers, hospitals and other community agencies negotiate relationships but do not design and manage these relationships with the view of an efficient system of care.

The hospital in the 20th century serves as the production facility delivering modern, technologically advanced care. This modern healthcare production facility symbolizes the community's aspirations for good health and relief from pain, but it is not the foundation for a system of care.

Within the walls of the hospital, the germ of a system exists in the relationships and communications between the physicians and other disciplines. In many respects, like a unique hotel, the hospital provides services for the benefit of patients while they are in the hospital but does not stretch this coordination and management outside the walls of the hospital and into creating a system of care in the community. Outside the hospital, however, there is little connection or coordination that would characterize a system of care between providers and services.

21st Century Continuum of Care Delivery System

The 21st century healthcare delivery system's continuum of care is built on the connectivity and interdependence of the organizations and services that deliver care at different levels of acuity to meet the diverse needs of individuals. Rather than pieces of a puzzle scattered around the community, the continuum of care in the 21st century fits together to deliver the services when the patient needs them and in the most effective and efficient way. This configuration is very different from the hospital-centric 20th century model that required the patient and the individual practitioner to piece together individual services to meet the patient's needs. In the 21st century, the continuum of care offers multiple access points open to the patient. With guidance, patients are able to select and access services that meet their needs. As patients utilize the services, the system monitors the points of contact and maintains the documentation so that the professionals involved in the care are able to coordinate the care and respond more effectively to the patients' needs in a more efficient and less costly manner.

Five possible characteristics for the 21st century delivery system continuum of care are as follows: (1) patients educated on continuum of care; (2) continuum of care with well-defined agencies and processes; (3) care coordination throughout the continuum of care; (4) agencies participate in a system that links care between providers; and (5) hospitals actively partner with agencies throughout the continuum of care.

As the healthcare system recognizes the role of patients as consumers, the system develops ways to guide patients in accessing and receiving services. As the first characteristic of the 21st century continuum of care, the importance of patients in the healthcare process requires that they understand the nature of a continuum of care and the way this system can be accessed and its services utilized. For patients trained in the importance of hospitals as the center of healthcare, this new perspective requires a reorientation and guidance that provide new images and understanding of healthcare as a continuum of care that corresponds to different states of health in the patient and incorporates different delivery models customized to best suit the needs of the patients. This approach places a priority on the patients and their ability to access and use the system. Just as the hospital became the center and symbol of healthcare in the 20th century because it was so visible as a part of life, the continuum of care as a model and a concept needs to become central to the understanding of healthcare for patients.

The second characteristic of the 21st century continuum of care looks at the change in the relationships within the care delivery system that occur in the future. Rather than independent businesses in which everyone is vying for patients, patients and providers recognize a well-defined continuum of care in the agencies delivering care and the processes used to deliver care. In this environment, the links between the hospital and post-acute care and from post-acute care to home and the outpatient environment are mapped and readily available so that patients no longer have to figure out the next step in their care. Guides to the continuum of care are available through materials from their doctor or hospital or online.

The processes of care in this new environment are logical and logically connected so that entry points and exit points and costs are clearly demarcated. The patient checks for the symptoms or the indicators for particular types of care and then contacts the agency for additional information or to access the care. Helping patients and their families to recognize these signposts in the care system and to determine where to go for help are key parts of the primary care relationship either online or at the primary care office.

Care coordination is the third characteristic of the 21st century continuum of care. Active coordination of care for patients serves as a key indicator of the future of healthcare. Since most patients are part of a local, regional, or national health insurance service, anytime they enter the care continuum, it is an important moment for the system that is responsible for the patient's care. Having patients randomly use services with no real guidance or coordination can result in significant costs that come back to haunt the system when the rating system evaluates system quality and efficiency. This makes care coordination an essential aspect of the care process.

Care coordination has always been a difficult task for health systems because it requires knowledge of patients and knowledge of how they use healthcare services. To manage the delivery of care throughout the continuum and to monitor patient access, care coordinators use electronic systems that link all the available systems and agencies with a system that indicates whenever a claim has been filed in the system. These electronic systems are the fourth characteristic of the 21st century continuum of care. Through these electronic systems, care coordinators follow patients within the system through registration records, care documentation, and claims generation. Through the use of predictive analytics, coordinators also determine where the patients may go based on demographics and medical history and intervene with the patients to guide them to the best care to meet their needs at the most appropriate costs based on their insurance plans.

The links in the healthcare continuum of the 21st century are not simply between the care coordinators and the agencies that deliver care. The agencies are also linked in the system and actively monitor the activities of patients and the types of services they use. As patients move through the continuum, the movement is part of the overall information system that links all the agencies. As the patients move through the system, use services, and generate claims, the agencies involved interact not only with the patient but also with other agencies in the care of patients.

For patients seeking care at an urgent care center, the local hospital receives information about the services needed and the care delivered. In leaving the urgent care center and going to the pharmacy, the medications provided to the patient are also communicated to the primary care provider listed for the patient. Following an acute care stay, the patient moves to a skilled nursing facility (SNF), and the primary care doctor is notified. When the SNF stay is over, the home healthcare agency picking up the patient, the primary care doctor, and the hospital are all notified of the movement of the patient. This is an example of the interdependency and communication that occur in the 21st century continuum of care.

Though the hospital retains a very important role in the healthcare continuum of the future, it is vital that the hospital does not view itself as the only player in the system. Hospitals must play a significant role in creating the information infrastructure and the quality oversight that establishes the basis for the operation of the continuum of care. This is the message in the fifth characteristic of the 21st century continuum of care.

In the 20th century, the hospital did not acknowledge its responsibility as a leading development partner in creating, operating, and maintaining the infrastructure of the continuum of care. In the 21st century, the hospital clearly understands the importance of its role in the system of care in the community and in the coordination of care. As the entity with the most sophisticated systems and the greatest resources, the hospital is an important partner for any agency interested in serving patients in the community. By working with the medical staff at the hospital to define and measure the quality of care delivered by the agencies in the community, the hospital can take an active role in improving the quality of care and supporting improvements in other agencies.

A vitally important distinction between the 20th and 21st century healthcare systems is the development and operation of a vast network of service agencies and providers that deliver care to the patients in the community. Back in the 20th century, the hospital stood alone, and other agencies clustered around it for crumbs. In the 21st century, the hospital has a leadership role in the creation, operations, and maintenance of the continuum of care. Not only does it provide much of the expertise, the infrastructure, and the resources for managing the system, but also it is the hospital's staff that monitor the actual movement of patients in the system and alert the medical staff whenever there are quality of care concerns. In this way, patients in the 21st century have the support and guidance they need to access the system, obtain the services that they need, and pay for those services through appropriate insurance arrangements. They are also guided to the most appropriate place to receive care with the system.

For healthcare organizations interested in transitioning into the 21st century, recognition of the structure, function, and importance of the continuum of care in the delivery system transition is a key indicator of progress into the future. The continuum of care represents a significant change from the past in

20th century hospital	Points (neg)	21st century continuum of care	Points (pos)
Patients view hospital as the place for care		Patients educated on continuum of care	
No clear picture of the agencies or processes of care in the continuum		Continuum of care with well-defined agencies and processes	
Care coordination only in hospital		Care coordination throughout the continuum of care	
Independent agencies deliver services without reference to other providers		Agencies participate in a system that links care between providers	
Hospital has limited communication with other care providers		Hospitals actively partners with agencies throughout the continuum	
Total (record on scorecard)		Total (record on scorecard)	

Figure 16.2 Example—Process transition delivery system characteristics assessment chart.

permitting patients as consumers to access care that they need and to receive guidance in managing their care with the continuum. All of the partners in the system must recognize their interdependence in the delivery of services and communication of patient activity. When there are breakdowns in the system, it is incumbent on the system to seek to remedy the disruption and to restore the services or connections. Training patients is a mutual responsibility within this environment as the ability of patients to use the services is critically important to curbing costs and improving outcomes. Payers and contracting agencies monitor quality and outcomes as they evaluate their participation in the system of care (see Figure 16.2).

Chapter 17

Process Transition: Information System—Isolation to Network

The third process transition is the information system transition (see Figure 17.1). This transition begins with the 20th century isolation category as the state of healthcare information system through much of the 20th century. The continuum of this transition ends with the 21st century network that reflects the growing connectivity and real-time access to clinical, decision-support, and operational information. Within the 20th century isolation category, healthcare organizations identify the characteristics in which their information systems continue to be hampered by limited connectivity between systems and limited applicability of the systems. In the 21st century network category, the healthcare organizations identify characteristics that indicate that their information systems have reached the point where all areas are connected, and the flow of information includes real-time clinical, decision-support, and operations information. Using the transition assessment chart, the sum of the columns based on the comparison of the characteristics indicates whether the organization reflects the 20th or 21st century healthcare organization structure.

The evolution of electronic information systems in healthcare is best described as a slow journey in which the information system transition moved from minimal computerization and limited connectivity with task-specific computers to information systems that linked all aspects of the healthcare system with clinical and organizational information widely available and with decision-support and analytics capabilities. The transition from fragmentation to connectivity is the story of the transition from 20th to 21st century healthcare. The expansion of data analysis on a massive scale led to the introduction of industrial quality into healthcare in the late 20th century as it indicated significant variation in the quality and cost of care.

System knowledge speaks to the accessibility within a healthcare organization of information about the organization itself. In the 20th century, the financial areas were able to gather and analyze large quantities of information to support

131

20th century information system isolation	Points (neg)	21st century information system network	Points (pos)
Total (record on scorecard)		Total (record on scorecard)	

Figure 17.1 Process transition information system characteristics assessment chart.

decision making and for organization planning. For people in the organization, knowledge about the organization was limited primarily to administration. In the 21st century, the organization and the information about the system are readily available and accessible because the demands of patients for efficient care require that workers be able to evaluate the actual pace of work and resources be available to accommodate the needs of the patients and to respond to interruptions in services. To meet patient and consumer demands, participation and dialogue at all levels are used to evaluate performance in real time and to respond to changes in the system quickly. The continuum measures for system knowledge are based on the ability of staff to access information about the system as well as their own work environments. The more this information is shared, the more employees integrate their work with the system as a whole.

20th Century Information System Isolation

Prior to the introduction of computers into healthcare, the handwritten paper medical record was the central repository of information about the clinical care of patients. Physicians, nurses, and other departments documented information in this medical record. This handwritten record shaped the workflows of staff and supported the central role of the physician in the care of patients by requiring all the information about the patient to be recorded in this one document.

The introduction of computers into healthcare began initially in the very large hospitals that could afford the investment and could justify the expenditure for processing capability to manage large databases associated with large numbers of patients. The areas of the hospital that required processing large amounts of relatively simple data such as finance, laboratory, radiology, and registration were areas in which computers first appeared. In the 20th century, data processing remained relatively simple and limited. It was not until the late 20th century that computers began to be linked to each other and to be developed into systems for sharing information. Isolated and fragmented electronic information system characterized the 20th century.

Five possible characteristics for 20th century information system isolation are as follows: (1) information systems isolated to departments and specific users; (2) data inaccessible outside department; (3) data difficult to interpret; (4) data do not support the work; and (5) information system does not integrate individual work with the system. These characteristics provide examples of 20th century information system isolation.

In the early stages of computerization, healthcare electronic information systems appeared in departments that needed to process simple data on a large scale. The laboratory, radiology, finance, and registration departments were among the first to see the benefit from the capture and retrieval of simple data on a large scale. This first characterization of the 20th century information system isolation identifies the isolated databases in which the hardware and software were limited to a specific computer in a specific place with only certain people able to access it. Specialized training to operate the system and to retrieve data limited the number of people able to work with it.

Within the limited capabilities of these systems, data storage and retrieval improved the efficiency of managing the data and demonstrated to the healthcare professionals the potential applicability of computer processing to tasks that previously required lots of time and staff. This was a significant step in an environment dependent on handwritten documentation and the central role of the hardcopy medical record. Introducing computers into this environment provided a striking contrast to the workflows of most of the 20th century, but computers continued to be limited in healthcare.

The 20th century information systems found in healthcare were islands in a sea of paper as emphasized by the first characteristic of 20th century information system isolation. Esoteric computerized data processing systems hidden in ancillary departments represented the first steps by healthcare into the world of computers. Interestingly, for a field dedicated to science and research and the latest developments, healthcare did not expand rapidly into broader adoption of computers. The data in the department-specific systems remained in the departments until clerical staff carried a single hardcopy printout of the results to the patient care units to insert in the patient's medical record. Printing hardcopy results of tests and manually inserting them in the patient's record were the original computer information system.

Beyond the relatively limited scope of the department-specific information systems, the reluctance of healthcare to broaden the implementation of computers into patient care areas grew out of the attachment to the hardcopy medical record. For physicians, this record written by hand and maintained as the true record of the patient's care represented an essential and familiar method of ordering and documenting care. It worked for the physician as a diary of the patient's hospitalization. Giving it up entailed a major shift in the way information was maintained in the organization and in the way the physician actually performed his/her work. Moving beyond the paper medical record to electronic information technology required significant changes in the workflow of physician and nurses and in their methods of communication; this change did not come quickly to healthcare.

The second possible characteristic of 20th century information system isolation points to the limited usefulness of the results produced by the first healthcare computer systems. In most cases, the result arrived as paper copies for inclusion in the paper medical record. The data on the paper required training to interpret and were of little interest outside of the individuals who created it and the very few who used the information. This limited exposure to the results of computerized information processes gave it the air of a very specialized activity that was foreign to the way healthcare worked. Like specialized testing that is performed only occasionally for a rare disease, the appearance in the 20th century of a page of computer printout was quickly stuffed in the paper medical chart and forgotten.

The third characteristic of 20th century information system isolation points to data that are inaccessible outside the department. Computer-generated information served very specific purposes for specific users. It was meant for a select few. Early computers operated in relative obscurity, which meant that most of the healthcare organizations did not benefit from the capability and did not recognize its broader application. Along with the prevailing view that the paper medical record was the appropriate form for patient information, the lack of widespread benefit from computer-generated information limited the early appeal.

The fourth possible characteristic of 20th century information system isolation points to the distance between the data generated in the individual computer and the work. Data available through the computers did not support the work due to the limited ability to access it and the way it existed outside the workflow. The method for generating data made it difficult to aggregate for analysis because the results arrived on paper and often disappeared into the medical record. The computer did not actually improve the work beyond increasing the efficiency of data collection for the individual department. For the rest of the organization, the computer in the lab meant one more piece of paper for the paper medical record.

Healthcare data affect the care of patients when the data contribute to decisions about care. Physicians and other care providers need the data at the time they make decisions. In the same way that data concerning the tolerance of a piece of machined equipment on an assembly line need to be available at the point of production, data need to be available at the point of care at the time that the care is delivered. In the early stages of data processing in healthcare, the data did not support the work in real time.

The final characteristic of 20th century information system isolation points to an important aspect of the limitations of the isolated information system. The information system does not integrate the individual's work into the system in a way that contributes to improving the work. Isolated computers feeding paper copies of results to the existing paper record become one more piece of paper in the isolated medical record. It was accessible only in one place by the people standing there and was only available so long as the medical record was there. Computers provide excellent ability to capture information and to store it, but it must be integrated into the broader system engaged with the care of the patient. The information must become part of the system for everyone in the system to benefit. This really was not possible in the 20th century prior to the development of network systems.

The integration of the work into a form that combines with existing data accessible across the system is an important part of building a system. An isolated computer is an island with limited ability to transmit and to receive. This creates impediments and limits the value of the data and use of data. As computer systems became more sophisticated, the connections and functionality improved. With this improvement, the value of the electronic health record became clearer, and people shared information and used it in the process of care.

Moving from the handwritten paper medical record to a computerized medical record did not occur in the 20th century. The introduction of computers into certain departments began the change. The computers of the time were limited in their capability and were difficult to access and use, and the data they generated were difficult to interpret. The hardcopy medical record remained foundational to the delivery of care. The results of the computer printout came too late for the care of the patient.

The isolated computers of the 20th century were effective testimony to the nature of healthcare and the dilemma that would develop as computers became more sophisticated. The attachment to the handwritten medical record remained embedded in the workflow and the consciousness of the physicians and other professionals as they delivered care to the patients. As electronic information systems became more sophisticated and capable of replacing the medical record, the process for changing workflows to use the computerized documentation rather than handwritten orders and notes was arduous and required significant investments of time and staff. This process exemplified the difficulties that healthcare professionals experience with change that interrupts processes that are repeated over and over again every day such as documenting patient care and writing orders. It is only in the 21st century that the reticence to let go of the paper record receded as the connectivity of electronic information system made the computer record truly useful in the care of the patient.

21st Century Information System Network

It is in the 21st century that the transformative benefits of electronic information systems truly appeared in healthcare. With these new systems, which are still in developmental stages compared to other industries, the workflows of healthcare change, and the value of connectivity appears. The importance of connectivity in healthcare for the concept of a system is indisputable but previously unrecognized. Healthcare in the 20th century had no sense of the desperate need for connections to make all the technology work, but the vision is forming as the information systems develop and begin to fulfill the promise that was latent from the beginning.

The technology is the first step. The technology that creates the connections to form the whole system links the data from the professionals to the patient and have it all come together at the right time and right place to support the right care. But there is an even greater challenge in the 20th century culture of American healthcare that was born in the handwritten medical record and continues in the shaping of technology to resemble the original medical record. Connectivity must transform the image of the medical record into a fluid, flowing, pervasive source of insight in order to remove the ghost from the machine and to build the future.

Five possible characteristics for 21st century information system network under the information system process transition are as follows: (1) information systems linked throughout the organization; (2) data accessible wherever needed; (3) data easily understood; (4) data support the work; and (5) information system integrates individual work with system. These characteristics provide examples of the way 21st century information system network differs from the isolation of the 20th century.

In this first characteristic of 21st century information system network, the connection is the point and the fundamental basis for all that comes next. The concept of connection is used because the information systems of the 21st century, though vastly improved over the 20th century, continue as multiple systems that are linked through interfaces. It is not one system. This is the future hope, but it is not the reality in early 21st century American healthcare. The initial transition to 21st century healthcare is a linking of all the data sources in a system. It is more than simply linking the departmental systems into a connect-the-dots type of configuration. The information systems in the 21st century must mimic human communication and thought processes by permitting the flow of questions, answers, and conversations between the system and the professionals and patients at the point of care. The speed of the flow and the availability of the information challenge the system to create a new experience.

In healthcare, the interaction between the patient and the providers takes place in real time. As noted in the second characteristic of 21st century information systems network. The conversation needs the latest data available to move the process of care at the fastest pace that is compatible with good care. In the 21st century, waiting for data is an inexcusable hindrance to the care process that frustrates providers and denigrates the experience of care. As processing capabilities increase in speed and the connections between data systems, the speed and accuracy improve.

The introduction of computers into the interaction between the patient and the physician or nurse represents a continuation of the long history of technology as an intermediary in the healthcare experience, but the computer takes it to a new level in the 21st century. In this new healthcare environment, the computer access transferred to a tablet is reminiscent of the ancient writing tablets. This tablet not only provides information but also overcomes the significant psychological problem of facing a computer screen rather than facing a patient. With the tablet, the physician and the patient have a conversation with the tablet serving as an advisor to the discussion. It is in this seamless flow of human conversation informed by the entire information system converging on a single point that the connectivity of the 21st century moves healthcare to the next level.

A screen full of numbers is an impediment to the conversation between the patient and the provider. The time required for the provider to sift through the numbers and draw conclusions is a delay that is not part of the 21st century care conversation identified in this third characteristic of 21st century information system network. To fulfill the 21st century promise of connectivity, the system must provide the analysis that converts the numbers into useful information.

The ease of understanding the data extends beyond the professionals to the patient. The patient is the ultimate consumer and determiner of value in the 21st century, and making information available in a form that answers the patient's questions is an essential part of this process. Patients will never have the training and experience to translate all data into actionable information, but the system needs to recognize the patient as a user of data and information by creating a framework for queries and responses that supports the work of the professionals and meets the needs of the patients.

As data move through the information system of the 21st century healthcare organization, the critical question raised by this fourth characteristic is the applicability of the data to the work. Designing the system with the goal of informing the work is an essential developmental aspect of the 21st century information system. This requires timely information delivered to the point of care and presented in an easily understood form that translates into actions within the care process.

For the healthcare professionals working at the point of care, the information system can either be an enormous source of frustration or a valuable ally. The application of the information presented by the system to the care process resolves this issue. As the systems become more sophisticated, the users move quickly to useful information and receive it in the form that helps in planning the next steps or responding effectively to the current problem.

The most powerful image of the 21st century information system network is an individual or a small group with the patient among them having a conversation. They focus on the patient rather than the computer. In their hands, they hold small tablets with illuminated screens. Occasionally, they tap the screen with their fingers, look up, and respond to a question that the patient asked a few moments before. Someone else in the group looks up from their screen and adds an additional comment.

In this interaction, the seamless flow of information into the care process as a helpful presence describes the vision that is 21st century information systems. The individual commands the system through a few taps on the screen. The network responds efficiently and effectively by searching out the data in the multiple databases that make up the system. It returns the information in milliseconds so that the answers arise within the normal flow of the conversation occurring between the patient and the healthcare professionals. This is the essence of the 21st century information system of care.

It was a long struggle, but in the end, the 21st century finally had its brain and nervous system in place to make all the computing power conceived in the 20th century available at the point of care. Connecting the multiple databases and systems with the point of care, the information system draws the data together and creates the platform to perform the role of advising the professionals and the patients and capturing these encounters and their results. The data are easily accessible wherever they are needed and are presented in a form that is easily understandable not only by the professionals but also on a certain level by the patients. The data speak to the care of the patient and help to guide the decision making with support capabilities that translate the various aspects of care into a unified plan that guides the team and informs the patients' decisions.

Finally, the system converges at the point of care and functions with the context of the individual or the group delivering care to the patient as described in the fifth characteristic. In the midst of this activity, the 21st century information system documents the work, serves as an advisor to the group and the patient by providing timely relevant information that answers the real questions, and structures the planning. This connected system brings together all the pieces of healthcare, human, and machine in a concerted effort to achieve the goals and to document the work.

The walls of the hospital and the distance to the patient are no longer impediments to the flow of information within the system. Essentially, time, space, and multiple systems merge into a process that is open to the patient, the care providers, and the organizations. This network of information incorporated into the services creates the healthcare system that is capable of delivering to the patients the right care in the right place at the right time to achieve the right goals at a cost that is sustainable. It finds its full fruition in the 21st century information system network.

The transition from 20th century information system isolation to 21st century information system network represents the transformation of healthcare from the individual physician in an office cutoff from patients to an information system with clinical databases, decision support, and real-time monitoring for all patients and practitioners. This transformation captures the essential element of the movement of American healthcare from the scientific machine to the complex adaptive system. The information system transition creates the network that transforms healthcare in the 21st century (see Figure 17.2).

20th century information system isolation	Points (neg)	21st century information system network	Points (pos)
Information systems isolated to departments and specific users		Information systems linked throughout the organization	
Data inaccessible outside department		Data accessible wherever needed	
Data difficult to interpret		Data easily understood	
Data do not support the work		Data support the work	
Information system does not integrate individual work with the system		Information system integrates individual work with system	
Total (record on scorecard)		Total (record on scorecard)	

Figure 17.2 Example—Process transition information system characteristics assessment chart.

Chapter 18

Process Transition: Financial—Fee-for-Service to Consumer Health Financing

The fourth process transition is the financial transition (see Figure 18.1). This transition begins with the 20th century fee-for-service category as the typical payment structure of 20th century healthcare. The continuum of this transition ends with 21st century consumer health financing that reflects the growing need of consumers to have access to more sophisticated financing options as they accept greater financial responsibility for healthcare. Within the 20th century fee-for-service category, healthcare organizations identify the characteristics in which their financial structure continues the process of individual charges for services with no incentives for reducing redundancy or efforts for assisting patient-customers in comparing costs and less-expensive alternatives. In the 21st century consumer health financing, healthcare organizations identify characteristics that indicate that their financial systems provide patient-customers with transparency in pricing, bundling of services to provide more accuracy in total costs, and methods of providing financing for higher-cost services. Using the transition assessment chart, the sum of the columns based on the comparison of the characteristics indicates whether the organization reflects the 20th century model or has progressed to a 21st century healthcare organization structure.

Initially, payment for healthcare services was either personal payment by the patient to the physician or philanthropic payment by wealthy patrons to charity hospitals to provide charity care to the indigent. With the introduction of operating rooms, laboratories, radiology, and professional nurses, physicians persuaded their paying patients to come to the hospital for care to take advantage of these new technological innovations. Hospitals provided services to meet the requirements of wealthy and middle-class patients and charged for the services.

With the evolution of insurance, employer and governmental, as the dominant payment process from the middle of the 20th century, payments were handled

20th century fee-for-service	Points (neg)	21st century consumer health financing	Points (pos)
Total (record on scorecard)		Total (record on scorecard)	

Figure 18.1   Process transition financial characteristics assessment chart.

through an intermediary. Service providers bill insurers, and the insurers pay specific fees for specific services with rates determined through negotiation. Hospitals and other healthcare providers designed the fee-for-service structure to provide specific charges for each item. This enabled providers to negotiate charges for services item by item and charge each time a physician ordered a service.

Patients as consumers in the 21st century will accept more responsibility for the costs of care and will have a greater role in decision making about care. They will demand more transparency in the actual costs of care. Consumers will need to know their total costs before they receive the services and to price packages of services to make it easier to compare prices between different providers. Health systems, insurers, and vendors will develop payment processes that involve sharing the risk of financial loss or gain and greater emphasis on the appropriate management of services and outcomes. As healthcare organizations become more sophisticated about their costs and care processes, they will take on more risks of potential financial loss or gain because of confidence that they can deliver care for less cost by controlling or removing redundancy and waste. At the same time, consumers will look for ways to obtain services for less cost and not depend on the insurers to pay for all services. Progression on the financial continuum involves transparency of costs for services, risk contracting, and population health contracting.

20th Century Fee-for-Service

In the fee-for-service world of 20th century healthcare, healthcare organizations deliver services and charge for each of the services that they deliver. Only a few organizations, such as Medicare, pay for services prospectively and depending on the diagnosis. For 20th century healthcare organizations, fee-for-service describes the primary method for the exchange. Within this exchange, there are multiple layers of negotiations between providers and payers of all sorts, but the basic model is payment for a specific service.

Five possible characteristics for the 20th century fee-for-service category under the financial system transition are as follows: (1) specific services ordered by physician, (2) insurance payments for specific services clearly defined, (3) payment based on delivery of service, (4) payment contracted on each specific service, and (5) payment unrelated to outcomes.

The 20th century fee-for-service process begins with the physician ordering a specific service or admitting a patient at the local hospital with a specific diagnosis. Within this arrangement, the payers and the service providers have an understanding of the particular services and the payments expected for the services. The provider of services delivers or performs the service and invoices the payer, usually an insurance company. The payer sends the payment. The patient is not involved as long as he/she has insurance. If the patient is uninsured, then he/she arranges for payment before obtaining the service unless it is an emergency.

The physician determines what services the patient needs and orders the services as indicated in the first characteristic of fee-for-service. The physician's order is the *sine qua non* for healthcare services. From a simple blood test to a major cardiac surgery, the physician writes the order, and the order authorizes the hospital to deliver it and the insurance company to pay for it. Without the physician's order, the system does not recognize the legitimacy of the request for service regardless of how appropriate it is except in emergencies.

In 20th century healthcare, most people do not directly pay for healthcare. Most people have insurance and use it to pay for their care. As the second characteristic of 20th century fee-for-service indicates, insurance pays for specific services. In a list buried in the insurance program documents, the insurance company describes products and services agreed upon in the negotiations that set up the insurance plan. This insurer pays for items included on the list and does not pay for items excluded. Specific services are covered and no others.

In the world of 20th century healthcare, identifying services covered by an insurance plan protects the insurance companies from medical costs that escalate quickly. This listing of specific services becomes the negotiation point between companies and insurers each time the insurance plan renews. Including more services makes the benefit better for the insured while increasing the risk to the insurer. Reducing coverage favors the insurance company. In this way, the insurance company works to reduce its risk of paying out more in benefits than it receives in premium payments.

In the third characteristic of 20th century fee-for-service, the healthcare organization converts the delivery of specific services in the hospital to a billable form for submission to insurers and other payers. This process begins when the physician orders the services in the medical record. When the patient leaves the hospital, coders review all the records and code the diagnoses of the patient; the seriousness of the illness; the tests, procedures, and care delivered to the patient; the time the patient spent in the hospital; and other information in the coding of the medical record by coders. The coders submit the coded items to the financial section of the hospital for processing and submission to the insurer. This payment process converts decisions by the physician into services that the provider delivers and then bills to the insurer. In this way, the healthcare provider delivers specific services, and the insurer pays for the services at the agreed-upon prices. Healthcare becomes the specific services delivered to the patients, and the insurers pay for the specific services the patient received.

As hospitals develop their means for obtaining payment from insurance companies, the hospital specifies the payment for each service based on the chargemaster listing for the service and the contractual agreement with the insurer. Hospitals create the chargemaster by itemizing every service and product to identify a charge for each. Hospitals include thousands and thousands of individual items and services in the chargemaster with specific charges attached to them. Using this listing, hospitals develop their fees for the services they deliver.

As described in the fourth characteristic of 20th century fee-for-service, insurance companies negotiate with hospitals to pay a percentage of charges on the items listed in the chargemaster. The hospital negotiates the largest percentage it can obtain and the mechanism for payment of specific services. When the patient obtains the service, the hospital bills the insurer for the service based on the agreement as a percentage of charges rather than full charges.

For the uninsured patient, the bill for care rendered by the hospital includes the full charge listed on the chargemaster for each item because no agreement exists between the patient and the provider to lower the charge, unless the hospital offers a charity or uninsured discount. Since hospitals negotiate with insurers based on charges for each item, charges change to improve payment as the insurers change their rates of pay for specific items. This is where the reality of the insurance-defined world of healthcare payment appears. Due to the negotiations between insurers and providers, the charges listed in the chargemaster often have no relevance to the actual cost of the item or service but, instead, reflect the distortions created by the insurer's contractual provisions negotiated with the hospital. Certain items have higher charges to take advantage of the willingness of insurers to pay more for a certain service. Full charges leading to much larger payments are the fate of the individual who obtains services without the benefit of the insurance's negotiated pricing. This is why insurance is the required payment mechanism for healthcare for anyone able to obtain it. Otherwise, hundreds of thousands of dollars in charges could fall on the individual because of a single hospital visit.

The final characteristic of 20th century healthcare fee-for-service points to the ultimate dilemma that afflicts healthcare. The payment of services has nothing to do with the outcomes of the patient receiving the services. It only addresses the delivery of the service. If the hospital delivers the service, and the patient died, the payment for the service is still expected. There may be specific provisions or qualifications on the delivery of the service, but the outcome has nothing to do with the payment.

The question of outcomes has been the essential payment question throughout the history of medicine and is the principle that shaped American healthcare's relationship with insurance. Unable to specify outcomes even between survival and nonsurvival, healthcare negotiated with insurers the specific services and the payments. There were no negotiations about the outcomes of the services and no guarantee beyond the service itself. For the provider, the goal was simply to provide the services in an acceptable way, and the outcomes were the concern of the physicians. If patients felt that the outcomes of care were unacceptable, they sought relief in the courts, but the providers and the insurer handled their arrangements separately from the outcomes of care.

The payment process for healthcare services defines an essential aspect of American healthcare that evolved during the 20th century. The physician and the hospital exist as separate components of the 20th century healthcare payment system. The physician's order is the basis for the delivery of healthcare services by licensure and by insurance agreement. There are no services and no payments without a physician's order. The physician orders the services, and the hospital had little control over what the physician orders.

Hospitals created hospital insurance as part of 20th century healthcare to enable patients to afford to come to the hospital. These payers identified specific services unrelated to the outcomes of care and negotiated with the hospitals and other providers on pricing. Since there are no predictable outcomes in healthcare, and since no hospital or insurance company is willing to predict the outcomes of care, the payer and the hospital negotiate on services rendered and services paid.

The charges created by the hospitals and agreed to by the insurers increased as the costs of equipment, staff, and facilities increased. Physicians ordered more, and the payment process of insurers and hospitals accommodated the increases by raising premiums to the employers and to the federal government. Without predictable outcomes to use in justifying the costs, there really were no limits except the ability of payers and the government to either pay for services or not.

In the end, fee-for-service encouraged the delivery of more and more services. Physicians had no responsibility for reducing costs and no way of ensuring the outcome of care, so they ordered whatever might help their patients. The insurers and the hospitals did whatever the physicians ordered and passed the costs on to the employers and the federal government. In the late 20th century, the costs reached a point that the entire system could no longer tolerate the increases, and the payers changed the rules of the game by beginning the care to produce acceptable outcomes, or there would be no payment. For hospitals, this was a game changer.

21st Century Consumer Health Financing

With the meter running very fast, everyone is looking for someone else to pay the cost of healthcare. Just as the demand for outcomes to justify the costs became the cry at the end of the 20th century, the 21st century initiated a search for a new payer. This search will ultimately lead to the patient. In the 20th century, as the healthcare delivery system evolved into physicians, hospitals, and patients, cost became the driver for hospitals. Physicians wrote orders based on what they thought would help their patients, and the hospitals delivered the services and then sought payment from the patients. When the patients could not afford hospital care, prepaid insurance offered a way to finance hospital care so that it would be available in times of illness or injury.

When employers turned to insurance companies to develop hospital insurance products, the hospitals and insurers created their own system designed to pay for services. Physicians retained the discretion to order what they felt the patient needed, the hospitals delivered the services, and insurers paid the negotiated rates and passed the costs to employers. The patients went to the doctor who admitted them to the hospital where they received the ordered services and either got better or died. The insurer paid the hospital regardless of the outcomes of care and essentially left the patient out of the negotiations and payments.

In the 21st century in America, government, employers, and insurers look to new payers to absorb the costs of a system grown beyond affordability. They hid the process of healthcare insurance in a black box and encouraged patients to follow their doctors' advice. The patient did not participate in the payment process. As the costs start to overwhelm the system, everyone believes that the patient as the consumer can save healthcare by making good choices. According to the employers, insurers, and federal government, consumers making good choices can save American healthcare by purchasing only products they desire and paying only what they choose to pay. Consumer health financing began with the call from insurers, employers, and the government for patients to become consumers in order to save healthcare from its cost conundrum. By unleashing consumers on American healthcare by shifting thousands of dollars of cost to them through high-deductible insurance plans, these empowered and incentivized consumers will change American healthcare in ways people did not anticipate.

Five possible characteristics for the 21st century consumer health financing under the financial system transition are as follows: (1) services ordered as part of evidence-based, established protocols involving all providers/vendors; (2) payment processes comanaged by patient, insurers, and providers; (3) payment amount negotiated based on service, quality, and outcomes for entire care process; (4) contracts establish criteria for payment based on service, quality, goals, and financing of total payments; and (5) payment contingent on outcomes that reflect patient goals.

Healthcare consumers do not understand healthcare or its payment processes, but they are the ones who are shopping for services in the 21st century. They are looking for services that they can purchase that will produce the outcomes they need at a price they can afford. Since healthcare delivery remains an obscure process directed through a complex system, the consumer shops for outcomes. These outcomes, like the purchase of any product, must be something that the consumers can recognize and understand if they are to buy them.

The first characteristic of 21st century healthcare consumer financing identifies the service delivery system as structured to deliver services in a predictable way based on established protocols. This is the product development aspect of healthcare to engage vendors and providers in using the best science to develop the services most likely to meet the needs of consumers. It follows the model of industry in looking to design processes that minimize defects and focus on producing value for the consumer.

Healthcare consumers are a major force in 21st century healthcare. As a payer, patients-turned-consumers need instruments that enable them to participate in the paying process. Insurers, physicians, and service providers such as hospitals will work together to create financial instruments as the second characteristic of 21st century consumer health financing.

Transparency of the process of pricing is the essential step that was never developed in the 20th century. In order to participate in 21st century healthcare as a major payer, consumers need to understand what they are buying, what it costs, and how they pay for it. For consumers, the payment process in healthcare is uncharted territory that payers hid from view in the previous century. A co-pay or deductible in a small amount is familiar, but managing thousands of dollars of costs for healthcare services is a new experience for an industry based in insurance. This level of expense requires a system that supports the financing of payments in the same way that consumers finance other services. All the participants in the care process work together to incorporate the payment process into the delivery of services so that it is clear to the patient how it works, what costs are involved, and what is being delivered in exchange for the payments.

As a consumer and a participant in the payment process for healthcare that the industry expects to control costs and obtaining care at better prices, the consumer must be at the table to participate in negotiations over charges. The consumer can no longer be a silent participant but instead be a significant voice in the process if it is to succeed.

In the third characteristic of 21st century healthcare consumer financing, the market becomes a significant force as consumers make selections based on price in addition to other consumer values such as convenience, accessibility, and quality of the services. For providers and insurers, the role of consumers as part of the market for payment products and healthcare services is a new factor that requires new approaches. With other services, consumers make their selections at the time of purchase, and this is new for providers and insurers. They trusted in established relationships. As convenience, accessibility, and price are factors for consumers making the choice for healthcare, the directed purchases of the past negotiated by insurers no longer drive the process. Even the direction of physicians does not guarantee that patients will purchase services.

Finally, and most importantly in the era of 21st century healthcare, the consumer needs solutions to problems or products to improve their health. Outcomes of care become a major factor in consumer choices for services. Talking with other consumers on the results of their care and their satisfaction is an important determiner in which services consumers select. Quality, service, and outcomes as well as the price weigh on the decisions that consumers make about healthcare. Consumers look for value as they understand it rather than the criteria professionals used in the 20th century. In 21st century healthcare consumer financing, the selection of services focuses on what consumers perceive as value.

In the past, the employer played a significant role in the selection of healthcare services and contracts, and services developed by providers and insurers focused on the needs of employers. This continues in the 21st century, but as the fourth characteristic of healthcare consumer financing, the way that consumers choose is often different from the choices made by others. Even within employer-designed healthcare plans, the choices of consumers play a significant role. If prices outside the network are lower, and if the quality and accessibility are better, consumers can choose to spend their considerable portion of the healthcare plan payment on outside services.

As part of the 21st century plan for consumer healthcare, companies and businesses want their employees to make choices that save money and produce better outcomes. With this dynamic at work, consumers within the company become important voices in the selection of plans, the pricing structure, and the satisfaction with the results. Insurers and network representatives can no longer assume that the employer is directing the care or that the employees will choose to use only the plan provided by the employer. Consumers spend their discretionary dollars where they perceive the value in their purchases.

Where outcomes were not the focus of 20th century insurance/provider negotiations, the goals of consumers purchasing healthcare services in the 21st century take center stage as they look for value in the outcomes that result from the services they choose. In this fifth characteristic of 21st century consumer health financing, the role of the patient as consumer is the focus, and the ability of healthcare organizations to identify and deliver particular outcomes is an important factor in whether consumers choose them for services.

The healthcare marketplace becomes the environment within which consumers compare products and services based on their goals. Providers compete in the marketplace by persuading consumers that they offer the best services. For consumers, the outcomes obtained by providers are a significant factor in the selection. For providers, the need to provide outcome information in addition to quality of services, accessibility, and costs makes this new market environment very challenging and different from the 20th century.

20th century fee-for-service	Points (neg)	21st century consumer health financing	Points (pos)
Specific services ordered by physician		Services ordered as part of evidence-based established protocols involving all providers/vendors	
Insurance payments for specific services clearly defined		Payment processes co-managed by patient, insurers, and providers	
Payment based on delivery of service		Payment amount negotiated based on service, quality, and outcomes for entire care process	
Payment contracted on each specific service		Contract establishes criteria for payment based on service, quality, goals, and financing of total payments	
Payment unrelated to outcomes		Payment contingent on outcomes that reflect patient goals	
Total (record on scorecard)		Total (record on scorecard)	

Figure 18.2   Example—Process transition financial characteristics assessment chart.

In addition to provider selection based on types of outcomes, consumers also look to providers for certain guarantees of services. This may include outcome management such as a guarantee to address any issues that arise within 90 days of a procedure. It may also involve guarantees related to wait times, responsiveness, communication, and other aspects of care that consumers value. For many consumers, healthcare as a service falls within the range of other services, and consumers expect healthcare to function like other services—only better.

In 21st century healthcare consumer financing, the relationship between patients, now consumers, and their providers and insurers shifts from patient compliance and lack of engagement that characterized the 20th century to a new and more active consumer role in the selection, payment, and rating of healthcare providers. For consumers, healthcare is a service like other services, and in the 21st century, this means that all aspects of the service delivery process must meet the needs of patients who have choices and who are encouraged to seek lower-cost alternatives (see Figure 18.2).

Chapter 19

Cultural Transition: Professional—Autonomy to Integration

The first cultural transition is the professional transition (see Figure 19.1). This transition begins with the 20th century autonomy category as the status of physicians in their relationships with other professionals and in their discretion related to patient care. The professional transition ends with the 21st century integration category that reflects the growing status of physicians and other professionals as integrated within the team and care structures of healthcare organizations. To use the professional transition assessment chart, identify five characteristics in your organization that fit the 20th century professional autonomy category, and document them in the column. In the 21st century professional integration category, identify five characteristics of professional integration in your organization that represent changes from the 20th century autonomy characteristics. Using the transition assessment chart, identify the dominant characteristic, the 20th or 21st century, currently in your organization, and assign a 1 in the column for that characteristic. When you have completed the assessment of the five characteristics in each category, total the columns, and document the totals on the transitions scorecard. The sum of the columns based on the comparison of the dominance of the characteristics indicates whether the organization reflects the 20th century model or has progressed to a 21st century healthcare organization structure.

Of all the transitions, the culture transitions represent perhaps the most difficult because they are literally at the heart of the way American healthcare conceives of itself. Born out of the 19th century industrial revolution and refined throughout the 20th century, these transitions are fundamental aspects of healthcare that are going throughout profound changes in the 21st century. The images that we associate with them reflect essential aspects of 20th century healthcare. They are the most inherently 20th century of the transitions and must change if healthcare organizations are to move into the 21st century.

149

20th century professional autonomy	Points (neg)	21st century professional integration	Points (pos)
Total (record on scorecard)		Total (record on scorecard)	

Figure 19.1 Cultural transition professional characteristics assessment chart.

The professional transition speaks to the professionalization of the physician that occurred in the 19th and early 20th century and shaped the role of physicians and the operations of hospitals in the early stages of their development. As healthcare coalesced around the physician and the hospital during the 20th century, the physicians through the structure of the medical staff in the local hospital and the national lobbying of the American Medical Association (AMA) had a profound effect on healthcare. This professionalization and the image projected by the AMA supported the image of the physician as a craftsman and a professional with unique skills that separated the individual and the profession from others in healthcare. The autonomy of the physician grew out of the historical context of the individual physicians caring for compliant and passive patients, and this image remains firmly entrenched in healthcare and the minds of patients even today (Leape 2012). There was no one else in healthcare who possessed the skills or the knowledge, and this gave the physician a singular role in making all of the decisions related to the care of patients. The individual responsibility of the physician for the patient, the legal structure of licensure, the healthcare fee-for-service payment structure, and the professional ethics of the medical profession all contributed to the unique status of physicians (Leape 2012).

The growth of physician professionalism in the late 19th and early 20th century was a significant factor in shaping American medicine because it created a standard for the autonomy of the physicians. Physician autonomy grew out of professionalism based on university education, state licensure, and medical staff privileges. This professionalism separated the physicians from the bureaucracy of the hospital and led to the creation of the medical staff as the professional association within the hospital defined by affiliations, peer relationships, and democratic processes.

The industrialization of healthcare challenges the 20th century model of the physicians as autonomous and pushes for an integrated team in which physicians play a leading role but do not have the unique status of arbiter of all decisions. In the 21st century, the autonomy and prerogatives of physicians change as multidisciplinary teams of care providers bring new knowledge and skills to the care process. The physician's role as an autonomous professional with unique privileges becomes an obstacle to the efficiency of the health system and to the work of multiple disciplines in the delivery of care. No longer is the individual physician in total charge of the care of patients but rather a team of professionals from a variety of specialties and disciplines joined together (Leape 2012). The availability of clinical information to a broad group of care providers undermines the unique status of one profession and shifts the view of healthcare from the physician to the patient.

20th Century Professional Autonomy

Events in the 19th and 20th century promoted the autonomy and the unique professional status of physicians. Evolving out of the struggle between allopathic or scientific medicine and the alternatives of naturopathic and homeopathic medicine, the technology that characterized the science of medicine boosted the physician as operating rooms were set up in hospitals along with x-rays and laboratories. The Flexner report further strengthened this status as many proprietary schools closed, and the Hopkins approach of university and medical school training dominated medical education with the help of the largess of the Rockefellers. Finally, the AMA promoted this status of the physician through the promotion of university-based medical education as the requirement for licensure by the state boards of medicine and for membership in the medical staff at local hospitals. Education, technology, licensure, and the efforts of the AMA structured medicine across the country with physicians as the unique professionals of the world.

Five possible characteristics for the 20th century professional autonomy category under the cultural transition are as follows: (1) separation of groups by professions; (2) visual designations of professions evident (e.g., white coat, white uniform); (3) professionals answer only to designated peers; (4) decision making based on professional status; and (5) social deference paid to particular professions.

Healthcare in the 20th century began with the physician as a singular figure, but it ended with a myriad of professions and specialties. The first characteristic of professional autonomy points to the historic evolution of healthcare professions and their resistance to a common vision that connected them. The physician and the slightly less accepted surgeon were the originals. Nursing arrived shortly after as a subordinate but nonetheless influential profession. As technology and research increased, surgery became the heart of the hospitals, and physicians exploded into vast numbers of specialties as they attempted to comprehend all the new knowledge and to maintain their unique market position. There was a tendency for these groups to view themselves as separate, and there was no compelling reason to diminish professional status or identity as long as each group performed its work well. The separation of groups by professions in the hospital emphasized the differences in their status and their work as they viewed the care of patients as separated into parts and each group owning a part. Each profession had its realm or niche, and they delivered their specialty to the patient they treated, but there was not a sense that the care between the disciplines needed to be coordinated or integrated.

Professional attire stands out as the second characteristic of 20th century professionalism that reinforced divisions between professions and the hospital bureaucracy in the daily operations of the hospital. The clothing of the professions made the members of the different groups distinctive in appearance and served as reminders of the rank and prerogatives of the various professions in their interactions and in the care of the patient. The most striking examples of clothing as professional designations are the physician's coat and the nurse's uniform. The physicians in long coats, typically black before the 20th century and white after 1900, clearly identified the profession as preeminent in any situation in which they appeared. In the same way, nurses in white uniforms with caps throughout most of the 20th century clearly separated themselves as a group from anyone else and established a professional, almost militaristic presence through their garb.

The hierarchy within the clinical structure stands out as the third characteristic of 20th century professionalism that tended to promote separation and autonomy. Each profession established its sphere of influence and levels of responsibility with clear demarcation of rights and privileges as a means for preventing usurpation of prerogatives and status. Individuals within the professions, particularly physicians, recognized accountability only to others they regarded as peers. The channels of communication followed the structure of the clinical and organizational hierarchy exemplified by resistance to critique by anyone not perceived of as a peer or of equal status in the organization. The organization often tolerated behavior in higher-ranking individuals considered unacceptable to others within the structure due to social standing or economic implications. The privileges of rank and recognition of status emerged out of the hierarchical structure of medical and nursing education that required deference to senior clinicians and subservience in the interactions between older and younger members of professions based on the craftsman model of the apprentice. This was particularly evident in the physicians and nurses.

For hospitals and other healthcare organizations, decision making in the 20th century is the fourth characteristic of professional autonomy. Patients viewed themselves as the patients of a particular physician, and the hospital viewed the patient as the patient of that physician. Clinical processes and physician decision making about patients flowed out of this perception. The structure of the organization and the organizational processes clinically and organizationally promoted the image of physicians as controlling the processes of care through orders and notes in the medical record. Physicians coordinated all aspects of care and served as the source of information about the patient and what was best for the patient. Anyone needing information or desiring to make changes in the care of the patients consulted the physician, and the physician ordered the change or rejected the suggestion. Access to patient information and the ability to issue orders and to command organizational resource followed the clinical hierarchy as it did the bureaucratic positions of power with the physicians in their various gradations followed by nursing and so forth.

Social deference as the fifth possible characteristic of professional autonomy naturally followed the organizational deference paid to the professionals as decision makers and revenue generators. The medical staff operated under its own bylaws, rules, and regulations that governed its structure and work. This separate structure supported the status and professional autonomy of the physicians. Nursing, though part of the organizational bureaucracy, maintained its own processes for addressing professional standards and issues. Any policies and procedures adopted by the organization that required physician participation were subject to review by the executive committee of the medical staff and even to a vote by the full medical staff in certain cases. If the medical staff rejected the change, and it affected clinical care, it would be difficult to implement.

As the hospital represents the blending of various groups into the care of the patients, there are numerous situations in which people from different groups work together. Within these situations in 20th century healthcare, the ranks of individuals within the organization carry significant weight in the discussions. The presence of clinical staff in meetings with their status declared by their attire often significantly influence discussions even when they are unrelated to clinical issues. This social deference in 20th century organizations exerted pervasive influence.

Depending on the issue under discussion or the individuals present, major decisions that affect patients and the organization and employees may hinge on the preferences of clinically important individuals and the cultural influence they exercise. Within the bureaucracy, the significance of this type of influence and the social deference paid to these individuals represent an important aspect of professional autonomy that shaped 20th century healthcare.

The structure and operation of the 20th century healthcare organizations modeled the scientific management of the industrial age in its bureaucracy and the professional affiliation in its medical staff. The professional side of healthcare organizations often maintained their separateness in relation to the rest of the organization and used this separateness to increase their influence and to create a separate status within the hospital. The separateness of the professions, particularly physicians, the unique attire, resistance to evaluation outside of peer groups, hierarchical decision-making prerogatives, and social deference in meetings and other group activities to the physicians all contributed to the sense of professional autonomy. The results of these indicators of professional status and the separation of the physician from the hospital operational bureaucracy and other groups resulted in significant power for the physicians even in areas not directly related to their clinical expertise or the care of their patients. The deference to physicians culturally divided hospitals and other organizations between physicians and nonphysicians. Because this cultural separation carried over into other areas beyond clinical, it shaped many aspects of healthcare organizations around the personal preferences of the physicians and reduced the focus on patients.

21st Century Professional Integration

The dominance of physicians in healthcare organizations is a hallmark of 20th century hospital structure and operations. In the 21st century, acknowledgment of the training and expertise of physicians and their significant role in creating the processes of care for patients remains very strong, but the separateness and professional autonomy of the 20th century have diminished. In its place is the integration of the physician into a multidisciplinary team in which many disciplines have a voice in the care of the patient, and the patients view themselves under the care of the organization rather than a single professional.

Integration can take many forms, but it begins with the sense in which everyone involved in the care of the patient is actively working with everyone else involved in the care process. Leape (2012, p. 6) describes integration as "the planned, thoughtful design of the care process for the benefit and protection of the patient." Leape (2012, p. 12) further describes the autonomous physician as "ill-suited to address the problems that many patients have today, where optimal solutions require collaboration, shared decision making and cooperative care management." It is clear that the integration of professionals, particularly physicians, into the collaborative processes of care represents the future of the care processes of the 21st century.

Five possible characteristics for 21st century professional integration under the professional transition are as follows: (1) all professionals are integrated into teams; (2) no special visual designation of professions; (3) professionals held accountable by the team; (4) all team members have a role in decision making; and (5) social deference to particular professions are not supported. Patient care in the 21st century no longer supports the 20th century view of healthcare as a lone physician in a hospital setting. In the 21st century, the breadth of knowledge and the number of disciplines engaged in the care of the patient are much greater than in the past. Each of the disciplines brings unique perspective to the patient's care, but each blends with the others to develop a comprehensive plan of care for the patients.

As the first characteristic of 21st century professional integration suggests, the integrated, multidisciplinary team is the production model for the 21st century and integrates the physician in a very different way from the role of the physician in the past. The 20th century placed the emphasis and all the responsibility for the patient's care on the physicians. Physicians were the autonomous decision makers who controlled all aspects of patient care. In the team model of the 21st century, the patient's needs and desires structure the care process rather than the physician serving as the sole reference point on the care of the patient. Using the needs and goals of the patient as the guide to the care process, the team develops a plan in which all the disciplines contribute to achieving the goals of the patient. The physician is the clinical leader of the team but does not exercise sole discretion in the work of the team or the care of the patient.

The second characteristic of 21st century professional integration relates to the visual cues that help to organize the work and identify care providers. In the past, attire identified rank within the clinical hierarchy such as long white lab coats as the 20th century emblem of the physicians. The attire for many professions and other staff no longer indicates rank as many different professionals wear long white coats today. Many wear scrubs in various colors, and nurses may even use colored outfits to designate groups associated with particular units or specialties such as cardiology or oncology. In the new environment, the emphasis is on the patient's need to identify the disciplines that care for them. Badges and other visual cues help patients to identify care providers and their roles. Status or rank no longer help in the delivery of care or promote effective work in patient care areas. It can even create distractions that slow down care or confuse the group working with the patient. Teams choose visual cues for their usefulness in the work of the team.

The third characteristic of 21st century professional integration relates to the team responsibility for the care of the patient. The source or reference point for the team is the patient rather than the physician or other clinical person, and the patient's progress or lack of it signifies the success of the team in the care of the patient. By focusing on the patient as the basis for accountability, the team members look to each other to achieve the goals established in discussion with the patient. The team holds itself responsible to evaluate what failed rather than looking for that judgment from the physician. Since the goals of the patients reflect more than a purely disease-focused application of technology or medications, the various professionals on the team and other members representing different disciplines bring a critical diversity to the care process that significantly improves the potential for achieving the patient's goals. Recognizing that patients are complex, and their needs are multifactorial, 21st century healthcare can no longer afford to depend on the views or perspectives of an individual practitioner or a single discipline to develop and implement care for patients.

The fourth characteristic of 21st century professional integration involves decision making within the team. Rather than an individual physician being responsible for all decisions, restoring health in a team-based care process involves multiple disciplines participating in decisions about the care of the patient. Accepting responsibility for the patient's care involves recognizing the dynamic situation in which the patient lives and the interaction of the disciplines on the team to address that situation.

As each of the disciplines brings to light their perspectives on the patient, a much richer and deeper understanding develops. The team draws on this richness to understand the immediate and long-term needs of the patient. Working with a plan developed in discussion with the patient and founded on the consensus of the team members, the team is able to bring together a comprehensive view of the patient's goals and to make decisions together to accomplish the goals in the very short time the patient is in the organization.

The ability for team members to share their knowledge, experience, and ideas requires a sense in which everyone on the team brings value to the work of the team. Anything that works against this sense of the value of each member or creates barriers to team members contributing to the work makes it more difficult for everyone to accomplish the goals of the patient and the team. It is within this context that the organization as a whole must view social deference to bureaucratic and professional status as counterproductive if it restricts the interplay of ideas.

The fifth characteristic of 21st century professional integration recognizes that expectations of social and professional deference work against the effectiveness of groups. Social and professional environments using a variety of values and signals create hierarchies that promote deference to certain individuals or professions. It is one thing when this status is an honorary status recognized by the organizations but quite another when individuals accrue to themselves the expectation of social or professional deference due to personal interests or inflated views of self-worth. Healthcare took this to a very high level in the 20th century by maintaining an extreme form of deference to the physician through most of the century even in areas not related to the clinical care of patients. Establishing the physician as predominate in all social engagements whether in committees, teams, or individually distorted the actual expertise of the physicians and shaped the care of patients and the operation of hospitals in ways that often simply supported the preferences of a small group rather than the work of the organization.

Shifting the focus from the physician to the patient and from the autonomous professional to the team opened up vast resources of creativity, knowledge, and experience for the organization to use in the design of systems and the care of patients. By creating a new understanding of the complexity of patient care and a greater awareness of the value that each discipline brings to the care process, the organization expands the conversation to include all the disciplines and the patient as well. This leads to better decisions based on more information and with the benefit of a broader body of research and knowledge.

The 21st century recognized the complexity of patient care in all its dimensions and realized the importance of addressing this complexity with a full complement of skills, experience, and talent. This new approach required a team with members from a number of disciplines able to work effectively together and with the patients. Because of the complexity of patient needs and the speed necessary to develop a plan and to execute it, 21st century organizations turned to team structures. Within these structures, disciplines come together with the patient to identify goals, develop plans, and produce the necessary results quickly.

Recognizing anything that worked against the effectiveness of the integration of the disciplines into a cohesive group, 21st century organizations identified the many elements of 20th century healthcare culture and processes that emphasized the dominance and autonomy of the physician role as counterproductive and distracting. The role of the physician remains very strong within the clinical

20th century professional autonomy	Points (neg)	21st century professional integration	Points (pos)
Separation of groups by professions		All professionals are integrated into teams	
Visual designations of professions evident (ex. white coat, white uniform)		No special visual designation of professions	
Professionals answer only to designated peers		Professionals held accountable by the team	
Decision-making affected by social/professional status		All team members have role in decision-making	
Expectations of social/professional deference permitted		Expectations of social/professional deference not supported	
Total (record on scorecard)		Total (record on scorecard)	

Figure 19.2   Example—Cultural transition professional characteristics assessment chart.

dimensions due to the structures of licensure, medical staff privileging, and other societal and legal aspects of patient care. However, organizations recognize that preferential treatment such as special attire, autonomous decision making, peer accountability outside the team, and social deference restricts collaboration and organizations' work to diminish vestiges of the 20th century. In place of the structures that supported the professional autonomy of the physician is the patient-focused team with consensus decision making and joint accountability. Organizational systems support the elimination of visual cues signifying power and the exercise of social and professional deference in favor of encouraging team members to participate and contribute to meet the needs and goals of the patients regardless of their profession, rank, or social status (see Figure 19.2).

Chapter 20

Cultural Transition: Metaphor—Scientific Machine to Complex Adaptive System

The second cultural transition is the metaphor transition (see Figure 20.1). This transition begins with the 20th century scientific machine metaphor as the dominant image of the hospital-based culture of 20th century healthcare. The continuum of this transition ends with the 21st century complex adaptive system that describes the nature of the healthcare organizations in which extensive information systems form the infrastructure for a complex system that spontaneously adapts to changes it encounters in its environment. Within the 20th century scientific machine category, healthcare organizations identify the characteristics in which organizations continue to be structured and to function with machine images as the model. In the 21st century complex adaptive system category, healthcare organizations identify characteristics that indicate that the image that most accurately describes the organization is the complex adaptive system. Using the transition assessment chart, the sum of the columns based on the comparison of the characteristics indicates whether the organization reflects the 20th century model or has progressed to a 21st century healthcare organization structure.

The metaphor transition operates on many levels in healthcare organizations, but the subtleness of a metaphor within the context of an industry or an organization makes it difficult to recognize the importance. For many people, the question of whether healthcare should be viewed as a machine or as a complex adaptive system makes little difference because it is what it is, and we need to work with it. However, the reality of this metaphorical shift is truly profound if the image of the organization as held in the minds and imaginations of the leadership and employees is recognized as a vital guide and motivational force that shapes the decisions and operations of the organization in countless albeit unnoticed ways. The importance of this transitional shift echoes in all the transitions. This transition, however, speaks to the overall perspective of organizations and healthcare

159

20th century scientific machine	Points (neg)	21st century complex adaptive system	Points (pos)
Total (record on scorecard)		Total (record on scorecard)	

Figure 20.1 Cultural transition metaphor characteristics assessment chart.

and describes the overall shift that other transitions support. This metaphorical transition guides the other transitions as they progress toward the 21st century.

A metaphor is the application of a concept or image to an unrelated concept or image to create new understanding. Metaphors are the way we understand the world and not just a figure of speech. Metaphors applied to healthcare shape our true understanding of healthcare. Metaphors applied to organizations shape the views of the organization and how it works. Metaphors are often invisible to us. Like the "light bulb of an idea" or the "leg of a table," they are part of our thoughts and speech, but we fail to see how they shape our understanding (Lakoff and Johnson 1980; Goodwin 2015).

Two competing healthcare organizational metaphors dominate the literature in the 20th and 21st century: scientific machine metaphor and complex adaptive system metaphor. The scientific machine metaphor is derived from the Newtonian view of identified causes and predictable effects. The expression of this concept organizationally becomes specific actions leading to specific results to meet specifically designed goals. The early 20th century view of the hospital as similar to a factory comes from this metaphor. The hospital becomes the scientific machine striving for efficiency with a bureaucratic departmental structure and a leadership structure based on hierarchical management directing and controlling all the work.

The metaphor of the complex adaptive system actually merges three organizational metaphors that Gareth Morgan (2006) identified as organism metaphor, processing brain metaphor, and flux and transformation metaphor. For American healthcare, these images can easily flow into descriptions of the state of healthcare organizations. With the implementation of information systems that create networks of employees in healthcare organizations, the processing brain metaphor creates an image of data flowing and many people processing it and developing information. As the information flows, it reaches many people, and as they react to the information and to the awareness of the organization and the environment, the organization functions as an organism in responding to changes. Finally, the complex structure of the organization grows as people interact and respond through their work activities and decisions and the thoughts and ideas they share. Through these interactions, the organization changes from one day to the next in its structures and responses. This flux and transformation arise in unpredictable ways through the ripples that begin small but lead to large changes as the network of people respond. In this way, Morgan's images apply to healthcare and help to define healthcare organizations.

20th Century Scientific Machine

As healthcare moved out of the family home and into the hospital in the late 19th and early 20th centuries to take advantage of the scientific discoveries associated with aseptic surgery, x-rays, and laboratories, a new structure began to emerge for the nascent healthcare organization to bring scientific management to the science of healthcare. This structure actually developed in industry, particularly manufacturing and railroads, before it migrated to healthcare. The idea was that a factory or a hospital was an organization in which different parts work together the way a machine operates and with the same efficiency. Administration at the top of the organization sends messages to the managers, and the managers direct the workers. The administration designs the work of the individual workers to be efficient and to fit the operation of the organization. With machine-like efficiency, each worker performs work under the manager's supervision. The manager reports the results to the administration. The image of organizations as efficient machines remained the dominant metaphor and the aspiration of administrators throughout the late 19th and 20th centuries. Hospitals like other organizations were to operate efficiently under the control of the superintendent or the administrator.

Five possible characteristics for the 20th century scientific machine category under the metaphor transition are as follows: (1) machine view of organizational operations, (2) clearly defined bureaucracy, (3) predictability of outcomes to plans monitored, (4) central control maintained, and (5) efficiency and correctness valued. These characteristics provide examples of the 20th century view of the scientific machine metaphor.

The final mechanical solution, the completion of the machine metaphor, appeared as the industrialization of healthcare in the late 20th century. The industrialization of healthcare broadened the metaphor of the machine beyond the support departments of the hospital that had always aspired to operational efficiency to the medical staff in the hospital. This new industrialization required that the product of the hospital operations, namely, the actual processes and outcomes of care, be efficient and produce quality commensurate with its costs. The medical staff, for the first time in the history of American medicine, is to be held accountable for the cost and quality of hospital production based on the same statistical process controls and outcome data that manufacturing uses to measure efficiency and quality of production.

The initial characteristic of 20th century healthcare related to the scientific machine metaphors is the use of machine image in describing work or the organization. Healthcare administrators trained in the 20th century in particular use the machine metaphors in common expressions in most organizations. The organization as a "well-tuned or well-oiled machine" is a frequently used image that directly relates to the scientific machine concept. Other less direct mechanistic images arise from industrialization such as individuals as "units," work as "processes," and the results of work as "product." Employees describing themselves as "cogs in the wheel" or "just a set of hands" give the sense of machine-like characteristics to employees and work along with leadership images of "driving the organization," "building a better mousetrap," and "plugging in the right parts" (Goodwin 2013, 2015).

The second characteristic of the 20th century scientific machine metaphor relates to the actual structure of healthcare organizations. Throughout the 20th century, the operational side of the hospital retained a well-defined bureaucracy designed to provide oversight and accountability for each function within the organization. The departmental structure with managers and directors over each function emphasized the specific positions responsible for each area and their role in directing the work to achieve the goals set by the leadership. This rational design lends itself to a mechanistic view of the organization in which there are control and predictable outcomes. The greater the emphasis on the positions within the organizational chart and the power associated with those positions, the more likely is the sense that the bureaucracy of the organization is designed to operate as a machine. By using the organizational chart to define authority, control, accountability, and communication, the leadership establishes a strong cause-and-effect image that functions like the diagram of a machine. The people in positions of power within the bureaucracy hold those below them accountable and answer to those above them. The expectation is that this diagram describes a mechanistic structure designed to produce predictable results if the structure functions efficiently and correctly. The view that by creating the structure, the organization should accomplish its goals carries the sense of the right parts in the right places and produces a machine that works well (Goodwin 2015).

The third characteristic of the 20th century scientific machine metaphor points to the sense of control or predictability in the organizations. Predictable results from the operation of the hospital are the reason for the carefully designed organizational chart and the usefulness of the machine metaphor in describing the operations. Like any machine, the organization of the hospital is designed to do specific work in line with the concept that the outcomes of the activities of the organization are predictable. If the leadership does its job, and if the workers do their jobs, then the organization will accomplish what it planned to accomplish. The ability to assemble the organization in a specific way to accomplish a specific purpose and then to see that purpose realized is at the heart of the mechanistic view of the organization.

For administration, in particular, predictability is vital. In discussions with governing boards and employees, management presents the vision of what the organization will accomplish with sufficient resources and if everything works correctly. Often, the governing board terminates managers or senior executives when their plans are not successful in producing the predicted results, and this incentivizes the leadership to cling tightly to the machine image that supports predictable outcomes. Working from these mechanical assumptions, healthcare administrators, CEOs, directors, and managers at all levels of the organization seek to assemble the machinery of production in the staff, the processes, and the facilities.

When the hospital does not produce the expected results, the machine metaphor represents a threat that someone failed to assemble the right parts or to operate the machine correctly. This view of failure as the failure of the machine or its operator assumes that the organization would be successful if only someone who knew how to run the machine was leading the organization. The expectation that predictable results are reasonable underlies the struggle in organizations between growing complexity and mechanical metaphors.

The fourth characteristic of the 20th century scientific machine metaphor relates to the central control that guides the organizational machine. Just as the organization as a machine should operate efficiently and produce the expected results, the direction of the machine must originate from the administration in order for the mechanical structure to work. Control at the center of the organization maintains predictability of outcomes from the machine perspective. Predictability diminishes with the loss of central control. In order to ensure achievement of the goals, the administration communicates to the managers throughout the system what they are to do to achieve their goals. The managers in turn are to communicate back to the administration what they have produced and how it compares to the predicted results.

Administrative control as the means for achieving results is derived from the view that a properly assembled machine will produce the expected results if the machine has the necessary direction from the central administration. Without this control to guide the organization, the various parts will not function appropriately, and the ability of the organization to produce the predicted outcomes becomes less certain. In the 20th century healthcare organization, the tight control of the administrative and clinical leadership on the operational side reinforces the right way for the organization to function.

Given the importance of control, the message from the administration to the managers directs them to recognize their accountability for achieving their portion of the goals. The managers in turn direct the employees to follow their procedures to ensure that the department or unit produces the right results within the parameters of the budget set by the central leadership. The employees follow the prescribed procedures and perform the work. It is not necessary that the employees or even the managers fully understand the direction and goals of the organization as long as they are producing the part they are assigned to produce.

The fifth characteristic of the 20th century scientific machine metaphor focuses on the purpose of the metaphor in producing results. The machine metaphor not only establishes a structure designed to control the operations of the organization and to produce results; it also provides the goal of efficiency and following direction as priorities. The efficiency of the organization relates to the way in which the parts work together in the use of resources and the speed of operation. Specific directions provided at each level through procedures guide the way to perform the work. Managers guide workers in following these standards with the expectations that it will lead to consistently good results that are produced quickly and with appropriate use of resources.

Following the correct procedures and achieving operational efficiencies are goals the organization celebrates. The administration identifies employees and managers who meet defined expectations using as few resources as possible as worthy of recognition and emulation. This represents the success of the machine metaphor and the leadership in building the right machine and operating it to achieve the goals of the organization. Frequently, these goals are financial and efficiency goals as would be expected of a well-tuned and running machine.

The 20th century hospital was born at the time when scientific management and the machine metaphor were in ascendancy. In the flush of the Second Industrial Revolution and at a time in healthcare when science was opening up all the secrets to life and prosperity, creating a well-designed bureaucracy in the hospital and operating it as an efficient machine seemed to be the path to delivering a new quality of life in America. As management embraced this new approach as more effective than the view of healthcare as a family enterprise, organizational charts with clearly defined leadership and departments and lines of accountability appeared as diagrams for the organizational machines. Employees received specific instruction on their work, and their managers were held accountable for work and for reporting to the leadership. Accounting and operational information provide to the central management guided future decisions on the areas that were not meeting expectations. Fine-tuning the operation by issuing directives to managers reinforced the role of the administration controlling the organization.

This model for the operational side of healthcare continued into the 21st century with only minimal changes. Administrators and managers followed it with an occasional nod to the role of employees in the success of the organization. The impetus to sustain and expand the machine metaphor came with industrialization of healthcare and the incorporation of the medical staff into the operations side of the hospital as payers demanded improved processes and outcomes like those in other industries. New information systems provided more data on operations and output and better tools for control. Expectations for predictable results expanded as well from payers tired of seeing cost increases with little to show for the expenses.

21st Century Healthcare Complex Adaptive System

Even as industrialization advances in healthcare organizations, the new metaphor of the complex adaptive system emerges spontaneously through the confluence of a variety of factors but especially the implementation of healthcare information technology and the appearance of patient-customers as a significant influence in the healthcare marketplace. Five possible characteristics for the 21st century complex adaptive system category of the metaphor transition are as follows: (1) complex adaptive system view of organizational operations; (2) complex system of relationships and communications create structure; (3) unpredictability, surprise, and discovery characterize planning; (4) adaptation and creativity encouraged and supported; (5) mission, values, and simple rules guide interactions that accomplish the work.

The first characteristic of the 21st century complex adaptive system category is the recognition that healthcare organizations are becoming complex adaptive systems as they implement and utilize information technology that creates the many connections between independent agents that define complexity. These systems provide clinical and operational information in real time to people throughout the organization, but more importantly, they enable the complex adaptive system to form through their ability to connect with each other. Out of these connections, individuals and groups share information, ideas, and feelings within the context of the work they perform. These relationships engender creative responses and unpredictable reactions to new situations that then produce additional unanticipated responses within the system. As these occur repeatedly through the organization, they create the complex adaptive system that actually becomes the organization.

The complex nature of the organization emerges out of the multiple interactions of people connected through the information system. At the same time, the adaptive aspect of the organization appears through the ways in which individuals and groups respond to changes in the environment and in the organization. Through interactions with patient-customers and communication between coworkers, new responses to changes, questions, and system issues appear without reference to higher levels of control. These new responses open up new possibilities for the organization to change and adapt as they are shared through communications with others in similar situations. Through this adaptive process, many people use and refine new methods of managing situations and new responses to changes in the community and in the needs and expectations of patient-customers. The adaptive impulse of the organization finds its application at the fringe where the organization interfaces with the outside world of patient-customers and the community.

As complexity and adaptation characterize the organization, the need for coordination and consistency is not entirely lost. In order that the ripples of adaptation that move through the complexity do not overwhelm the connections that hold the organization together, the system aspect provides the cohesion. In the minds and thoughts of the individuals engaged in the communications and adaptation of the organization, they share a common mission, values, and simple rules that form the system context for the complex adaptive system. As they encounter new situations or receive new communications that require rapid responses, the individuals throughout the organization reflect on the mission that binds them together and the values that they share and believe. Based on these fundamental views of the reason for the organization and the values that it espouses as good and right, they share simple rules as they perform their work. These simple rules serve as operational guides that enable them to respond quickly and to react with confidence to new situations. In this way, the organization operates at the speed and level of complexity that permits it to adapt and find the fit that enables it to meet the expectation of its employees and to exceed the expectations of the patient-customers who look for rapid results to complex issues.

The second characteristic of the 21st century complex adaptive system metaphor category highlights the complex system of relationships and communications that create the structure of the organization. This new environment creates the organization based on relationships rather than accountability and control. As patient-customers and employees share information with each other and with others, the ripples produce changes that lead to new connections and relationships. In fact, the nature of the organization transforms as the conversations occur, and new perspectives appear. If there are sufficient conversations, and sufficient numbers of people recognize the changes as helpful, change continues until it becomes part of the normal processes. Out of the conversations and the responses to the conversations, a new organization begins to form in very subtle ways.

In the third characteristic of the 21st century complex adaptive system category, unpredictability, surprise, and discovery form the planning processes of the organization. Where the scientific machine emphasized control and predictability within a static universe of immutable laws, healthcare in the 21st century thrives within an environment of unpredictability in all its operations. Regardless of the due diligence encouraged by the legal and managerial aspects of the organization, unpredictability lies innate within any situation or plan. No amount of planning and conditioning can remove all the potential combinations of variables that come together in any plan. In place of the fear that comes naturally with lack of control, complex adaptive systems recognize the illusion of control and the benefit that comes with abandoning the illusion.

With no illusion of control, a new openness to surprise and discovery characterizes organizational planning and change. Surprise arises naturally, as the implementation of new plans provokes responses not anticipated in the planning. Out of these responses from the system, the potential for discovering more insights and additional opportunities for change and improvement appear. It is in this combination of recognizing the unpredictable and looking to be surprised with new discoveries that organizations enjoy the benefits that arise from their nature as complex adaptive systems. In this way, 21st century healthcare organizations look forward to discovering new ways to operate with surprise, a natural occurrence from the unpredictability that occurs whenever the system encounters a new plan or new situation.

The fourth characteristic of the 21st century complex adaptive system category recognizes the inherent nature of adaptation and creativity as part of complex systems engaged and interacting with the environment and internal changes and promotes these as essential system qualities. Adaptation and creativity in managing changes play to the strengths of 21st century healthcare in opening opportunities to reimagine the nature of healthcare and its expression in organizations. The healthcare environment that tended to be so static for much of the 20th century now changes quickly and frequently with multiple new influences and new perspectives conspiring to undermine the perception of stability. In reality, organizations require adaptation and creativity on a continuous basis in order to maintain their fit with an environment in flux due to the demands of patient-customers and payers and expanding flow of information.

Adapting to a continuously changing environment externally and internally represents a significant challenge for 21st century healthcare organizations. Many of the changes arise from patient-customers and changing situations in the marketplace of healthcare. Others arise from regulatory agencies and changes in laws. Internally, the organization itself spontaneously adjusts and adapts as new services develop, and older services change or disappear. All of these changes and the associated responses form an ongoing adaptive response by the organization to aligning and realigning itself with the environment in which it must exist.

The fifth characteristic of the 21st century complex adaptive system category points to the need to operationalize the ability of the organization to grow and respond effectively. Mission, values, and simple rules guide interactions that accomplish the work and enable the organization to respond to changes and to embrace the environment as key to its own success. Each change that occurs creates new opportunities for growth and greater insight into the delivery of services. To take advantage of these opportunities, the organization must free its employees to interact, to respond quickly, and to share information freely. It is out of these interactions and the sharing of information that sufficient numbers of people join in formulating a new approach that adapts to the new environment. Based on the mission, values, and simple rules, employees have the tools they need to guide the interactions and to provide parameters for decisions. This basis for action recognizes the vital importance of the relationships and communications that occur in the 21st century organization. The mutual support and collaboration by the individuals and groups within the organization that grow out of the common understandings of the mission, vision, and values are the strength of the organization. Out of this context, employees recognize that it is within their ability at all levels to engage with the environment and each other with a sense of their personal value and ability to contribute.

Collaboration at the microlevels and macrolevels is critical to facilitate the adaptive response to changes as well as to accomplish the work that is required each day. In a fluid environment, the organization needs people engaged in the process of experiencing what is happening and developing ideas for adapting to what is happening. In sharing these perspectives and ideas with others, the organization expands its awareness and begins to develop a broader spectrum of options for responding. The celebration of this work and this mutual support within the system builds the capacity of the organization to absorb new ideas and to respond quickly and effectively to the opportunities that present themselves.

The metaphor of the complex adaptive system arises in healthcare organizations as information systems expand and connect the people in the organization in new ways. The complexity resides in the connections that develop between

20th century scientific machine	Points (neg)	21st century complex adaptive system	Points (pos)
Scientific machine view of organizational operations		Complex adaptive system view of organizational operations	
Clearly-defined bureaucracy		Complex system of relationships and communications creates structure	
Predictability of organizational outcomes compared to plans		Unpredictability, surprise, and discovery characterize the plan	
Central control maintained		Adaptation and creativity encouraged and supported	
Efficiency and correctness valued		Mission, values, and simple rules guide interactions that accomplish the work	
Total (record on scorecard)		Total (record on scorecard)	

Figure 20.2 Example—Cultural transition metaphor characteristics assessment chart.

the individuals and groups in the organizations. As information flows more freely, and more people have access to the information, they share what they know with others, and they share their thoughts and ideas. As enough people respond to changes, and enough conversations occur about the need for an effective response, new responses appear, and the organization begins to adapt to the changes that are occurring.

Relationship takes the place of command and control, and conversations take the place of meetings. Flexibility and simple rules guide the process of the organizations, and employees at all levels feel that they have the ability to identify changes, develop ideas, and collaborate with others in the organizations on refining and implementing the ideas. The focus is on the flow of information between the organization and its patients and customers and within the organization. With each additional piece of information and each interaction, the people involved are able to add to the common knowledge of the organization and to work with others to consider how this knowledge opens up new opportunities for better services, increased efficiency, and greater success for the patients, the customers, and the organizations (see Figure 20.2).

FOLLOWING THE MAP TO 21ST CENTURY HEALTHCARE

Chapter 21

Signposts and Motivation for the Journey

In following the map to 21st century healthcare, healthcare organizations striving to reach the goal need guidance and motivation along the way. They need guidance because the demands of operating in a rapidly changing environment make it easy to lose sight of the goals while taking care of the more pressing issues each day. They need motivation to invest energy and effort in the journey when the future often seems a distant concern and less urgent and meaningful than working on the current problems. The signposts and the motivation to continue the journey come from continuously referencing back to the transitions and the images of the future that they provide.

The ten transitions provide not only a measure for assessing progress along the way; they also guide the continuing effort through the images of the future that is the goal. The 21st century categories of the transitions side by side with the 20th century images serve as reminders that the future is different from the current healthcare world. The constant comparison between the images of healthcare in the past and in the future serves to reinforce the motivation that initiated the journey and the need to continue moving forward. In providing constant references to the past, the future, and the need to persevere, the transition as generative metaphors guide and motivate healthcare organizations in their journey to 21st century healthcare.

In the organization transitions, healthcare organizations focus on the move from the hierarchy structure of the 20th century to the complex system of the 21st century. Finding ways to recognize and use the flexibility and agility of complexity guided by the mission, values, and simple rules provides healthcare organizations with the ability to respond quickly to changes and to shift as the environment around them continuously evolves. In the midst of these changes, however, the organizations maintain their focus and cohesion because the mission, values, and simple rules of the systems work as daily points of reference binding the parts together in a common sense of purpose and direction.

171

Within the new structure, the relationship between the employees and the organizations moves forward from specific tasks and transactional agreements to the emergence of the work as employees use all their creativity and skills to meet the needs of patient-customers and their coworkers. Working together to respond to new challenges every day, employees confidently create their work and their sense of the work as they interact with patient-customers and share new ideas with coworkers. No longer bound to rigid rules that define the work of the past, they move forward to discover and create the work of today and tomorrow with the mission, values, and simple rules as their guides.

Leadership within the organization transitions moves from the need to control out of fear of loss or desire for prestige to empowerment that comes from trust and a common understanding of the mission, values, and simple rules that guide the work. With the support of positional power and trusting their common points of references, employees function as leaders whenever the situation and the interactions with coworkers create the opportunity and need. Rather than a title and position, they discover leadership and followership through their interactions, and they move forward quickly instead of waiting for permission and direction. With simple rules, the mission, and values as points of reference, employees experience a new boldness that comes from trust and confidence that they can lead or follow depending on the situation. No longer defending a static sense of place or position, leadership appears wherever the situation creates the need for it and complements the desires of others to follow and support the direction forward.

As employees discover their work and exercise leadership within the complex system of future healthcare organizations, they find new opportunities to innovate as a daily part of their work and their discussion with others. Innovation no longer resides in the positions of power or a central structure, but it now arises as an adaptive response of the employees within the complex system in its moment-by-moment interactions with the environment and the internal dynamics of the organizations. Drawing on their implicit understanding of work developed through experiences in actually performing the work and combining this with their personal commitment to the mission and values of the organization, employees discover new ways to work as they encounter new situations and needs. They share these discoveries with others in conversations and discussions as a spontaneous spread of innovation that helps others to adapt to the changes occurring around them.

The 21st century categories of the organization transitions offer healthcare organizations the vision they need to guide them to the future. The 20th century categories provide the motivation to persevere on the journey by serving as the organizational memory of just how far they have come. The past formed the basis for the journey, but it is in the visions of the future that healthcare organizations find the hope to successfully meet the challenges that confront them in the organization transitions.

The process transitions offer reminders in the categories of the 20th century that healthcare can no longer survive in the ways of the past because the demands of the marketplace require lower costs and higher quality. In the images of the future, healthcare organizations find their guidance toward processes that provide patient-customers with access to all the services they need and the costs, quality, and convenience they expect. The images of the past and the future within the process transitions serve as guides and motivators to continue the journey.

The lone physician sitting beside the bed impotently awaits the crisis to pass for a little girl as her parents stand in the background served as the ideal of the physician in the past. This craftsman image of the physician that stirred the imagination of healthcare in the past no longer inspires hope or offers an ideal to follow. The multidisciplinary team of healthcare professionals responds vigorously in a creative interaction with the patient-customer to identify the needs and to create the goals that will guide the care process. Drawing on multiple disciplines and sophisticated technology, this image of a team shaped by the goals of the patient-customer powers the future of healthcare and the processes of care.

Though the hospital of the 20th century stood as a fortress on the hill defending the village from illness, injury, and death, the image of the future is no longer this solitary image of a stable institution. The healthcare delivery system of the future draws together a broad spectrum of services and diverse delivery system in a continuum of care designed to meet the needs and expectations of patient-customers. Constantly evolving as new technology develops and patient-customers express new preferences, the future continuum of care offers services, from simple information to lifesaving intensive care, with greater convenience and easier access.

Supporting this new image of a dynamic continuum of care is the image of an information system linking all the points of care together in a common record and common network that supports the care providers and patient-customers. Looking back at the 20th century images of paper records written by hand and the isolated computer in a backroom, healthcare organizations respond to the pull of the future and struggle through the many obstacles to create the information infrastructure that supports healthcare in the future. The vision of connectivity and seamless information flow help to maintain the focus on the potential that lies ahead for healthcare and their patient-customers in the network of the future.

The financial darkness of the 20th century presents a frightening image of healthcare in America as available only to certain groups and an insurance-driven, fee-for-service anything-goes environment that created the fortresses and palaces. The 21st century image focuses on the patient-customer rather than the professionals and the institutions and turns to the familiar structures of the market to create a new way to access care. As patient-customers assume their role as the true customers of healthcare, the ability of healthcare to find ways to support health financing offers hope that the crisis-based acute care of the 20th century will be a distant memory as the health financing of the future supports a new way of life for patient-customers.

Out of all the transitions, the cultural transitions offer the images of transformation. Whereas the 20th century supported the exalted professionalism of the autonomous scientist and artist wielding amazing knowledge and exercising complete control, the image of the 21st century finds these skills and knowledge integrated into a deeper, richer creative enterprise. In this new world that is just beginning to appear, the best and the brightest come together with patient-customers to develop a plan that coordinates all the elements of the continuum of care around a common goal. The culture of deference to individuals that institutions and society taught and supported in the 20th century no longer represents the values or meets the needs of the patient-customers or healthcare in the future. The 21st century finds its highest expressions of wisdom and knowledge within the context of the combined intelligence of the team that commits to the welfare of the patient-customers rather than the prestige of the individual practitioner.

The metaphor embraced by 20th century healthcare looked to the scientific machine as the aspiration of healthcare organizations. Healthcare as a scientific enterprise operated as an efficient machine designed to deliver the most efficient care under the control of trained administrators and scientist physicians. Healthcare organizations find themselves struggling to fulfill this image today as industrialization advances into the clinical areas that avoided it in the rarified professionalism of the past. Having failed at controlling costs and delivering quality, the image of the scientific machine roared to life at the end of the 20th century to bring healthcare into the present age, but this image is not the end.

The disciplining of healthcare through industrialization proceeds today, but the image of the 21st century slowly beginning to appear as expressed in all the transitions is a complex adaptive system that is much less a scientific machine and much more a dynamic, living enterprise rediscovering its purpose and creating itself every day. With the vestiges of the 20th century cauterized by industrialization, healthcare in the 21st century will assume new structures and new perspectives that will emerge out of the changes that are in motion today. It is this vision that truly challenges and transforms healthcare organizations to embrace the transitions and to build the consensus for mapping the path to 21st century healthcare.

Chapter 22

Next Steps

Welcome to the next steps. Whether you are someone in healthcare, someone who uses healthcare, or someone who is simply interested in healthcare, your first thought at the end of this book is whether you have seen a transition lately. You may even start looking for them in your healthcare organization, in your next visit to your favorite healthcare provider, or anywhere else you see something related to healthcare. Taking a more systematic approach, there are some next steps that can be useful.

The first step involves industrialization. If you are in some way involved with a healthcare organization, you are familiar with the proliferation of data that seems to be everywhere today. Everyone seems to be collecting data on patients, processes, outcomes, and almost everything measurable in healthcare. The appearance of all the data plastered on walls, websites, and magazines is part of the effort by the government, industry, and advocacy groups to find ways to reduce costs and improve quality in healthcare. For healthcare organizations, all the data are creating lots of angst to appear to do well but struggling to figure out how to do it and what it means. All the data are a sign that industrialization is happening in the healthcare world, but the industrialization that brings the transitions to light is more than capturing and reporting data.

Industrialization begins in healthcare organizations when the pressure to perform well on all the data reaches a crisis point. This crisis typically occurs either because the organization is not doing well on its measures, or the organization fears that other healthcare organizations will charge ahead with Lean, Six Sigma, or another industrial quality method. In either case, the move to industrialization is the first step toward 21st century healthcare. This step is necessary because the 20th century parts of the healthcare organizations remain buried until industrialization forces them to appear. The 20th century aspects of the organization cause it to do poorly on the measures and keep it from improving as rapidly as it should. Industrialization forces these aspects of the organizations out into the open because they directly conflict with the values and practices of industrial quality.

175

If you are wondering if your organization has begun industrialization, use the industrialization assessment to get a quick sense of where it stands. If you have many fives, you may already be moving into the level of industrialization that leads to the next step. If you have few fives, you are probably not there yet, and industrialization needs to begin. There are many ways to begin it, but knowing that you need to begin is your first step.

Once industrialization begins in earnest in all parts of the organization, including the clinical areas, the next step is to look for the transitions that begin to appear. The transitions appear as the industrialization provokes conflicts with the 20th century elements of the organization. This does not happen immediately or automatically because many organizations may not be able to industrialize to the point that conflicts appear. The traditions, practices, and values of 20th century healthcare deeply embedded in many organizations represent a powerful core that may successfully resist industrialization and prevent it from progressing.

If industrialization does progress, conflicts with 20th century healthcare practices, traditions, and values escalate to the point that the organization cannot retain the 20th century practices and continue to progress with industrialization. At this point, images of the 21st century future begin to appear as alternatives to the 20th century images that are resisting industrialization. This is when the categories of the transitions begin to make sense, and applying them to the organization sets up the transition assessment charts to evaluate progress toward the 21st century end of the transitions.

Once the organization begins to use the transition assessment charts and other assessment tools, the implementation of industrialization has reached a point that it is now part of the organization. The industrialization continues as a normal part of operations for the organization. The transitions now become the basis for guiding the organization forward by building consensus on the images of the future and the steps needed to realize these images. The transitions also serve as motivation in encouraging employees in the organization to see the 21st century images as the direction forward and to want to go in that direction.

References

American College of Surgeons. 2006. *The 1919 Minimum Standard Document.* Available at https://www.facs.org/about%20acs/archives/pasthighlights/minimumhighlight.

Barrett, F. and D. L. Cooperrider. 1990. Generative metaphor intervention: A new approach for working with systems divided by conflict and caught in defensive perception. *The Journal of Applied Behavioral Science* 26 (2), 219–239.

Bernard, T. S. 2014. High health plan deductibles weigh down more employees. *New York Times.* (September 1). Available at http://www.nytimes.com/2014/09/02/business/increasingly-high-deductible-health-plans-weigh-down-employees.html?_r=0.

BusinessDictionary.com. Available at http://www.businessdictionary.com.

Berwick, D. M., A. B. Godfrey, and J. Roessner. 1990. *Curing Healthcare: New Strategies for Quality Improvement.* San Francisco: Jossey-Bass Publishers.

Dartmouth Health Atlas. 2014. Available at http://www.dartmouthatlas.org/.

Dictionary.com. Available at dictionary.reference.com.

Dobyns, L. and C. Crawford-Mason. 1991. *Quality of Else.* Boston: Houghton and Mifflin.

Donabedian, A. 1980. *The Definition of Quality and Approaches to Its Assessment.* Ann Arbor, MI: Health Administration Press.

Galbraith, A. A., D. Ross-Degnan, S. B. Soumerai, M. B. Rosenthal, C. Gay, and T. A. Lieu. 2011. Nearly half of families in high-deductible health plans whose members have chronic conditions face substantial financial burden. *Health Affairs* 30 (2), 322–331.

Gilbreth, F. B. 1914. *Scientific Management in the Hospital.* Speech delivered at the American Hospital Association, St. Paul, Minnesota. Retrieved 8/24/2012. Available at https://engineering.purdue.edu/IE/GilbrethLibrary/gilbrethproject/mgmthospitals.

Goldratt, E. M. 1999. *Theory of Constraints.* Great Barrington, MA: North River Press.

Goodwin, C. S. 2013. *Healthcare Organizational Metaphors and Implications for Leadership.* D.A. diss. Franklin Pierce University. Proquest (3567804). Available at http://gradworks.umi.com/35/67/3567804.html.

Goodwin, S. 2015. *Transition to 21st Century Healthcare: A Guide for Leaders and Quality Professionals.* Boca Raton, FL: CRC Press.

Harry, M. and R. Schroeder. 2000. *Six Sigma: The Breakthrough Management Strategy Revolutionizing the World's Top Corporations.* New York: Doubleday.

Harvard Business Review Reprint F14092 (HBR) 2014. *September Vision Statement: The Chart that Organized the 20th Century,* pp. 32–33.

Hospital Quality Initiative Overview Centers for Medicare and Medicaid Services. 2008 (July). Available at https://www.cms.gov/Medicare/Quality-Initiatives-Patient-Assessment-Instruments/HospitalQualityInits/index.html?redirect=/HospitalQualityInits/30_HospitalHCAHPS.asp.

178 ■ *References*

Hounshell, D. A. 1984. *From the American System to Mass Production, 1800–1932.* Baltimore: The Johns Hopkins University Press.

Howell, J. D. 1995. *Technology in the Hospital: Transforming Patient Care in the Early Twentieth Century.* Baltimore: The Johns Hopkins University Press.

Institute of Medicine (IOM). 1999. *To Err Is Human: Building a Safer Health System.* Washington, DC: The National Academies Press.

Institute of Medicine (IOM). 2001. *Crossing the Quality Chasm: A New Health System for the 21st Century.* Washington, DC: The National Academies Press.

Institute of Medicine (IOM). 2012. *Best Care at Lower Cost: The Path to Continuously Learning Health Care in America.* Washington, DC: The National Academies Press.

Institute of Medicine (IOM). 2013. *Variation in Health Care Spending: Target Decision Making, Not Geography.* Washington, DC: The National Academies Press.

Kenney, C. C. 2008. *The Best Practice: How the New Quality Movement Is Transforming Medicine.* New York: Public Affairs.

Lakoff, G. and M. Johnson. 1980. *Metaphors We Live By.* Chicago: The University of Chicago Press, Inc.

Lindberg, C., S. Nash, and C. Lindberg. 2008. *On the Edge: Nursing in the Age of Complexity.* Bordentown, NJ: Plexus Press.

Lohr, K. N. ed. 1990. *Medicare: A Strategy for Quality Assurance, Volume 1.* Committee to Design a Strategy for Quality Review and Assurance in Medicare, Institute of Medicine. Washington, DC: The National Academies Press.

Lucian Leape Institute Roundtable on Care Integration. 2012. *Order from Chaos: Accelerating Care Integration.* Available at http://c.ymcdn.com/sites/www.npsf.org /resource/resmgr/LLI/Order_from_Chaos_final_web.pdf.

Merriam-Webster Online Dictionary. Available at http://www.merriam-webster.com.

Morgan, G. 1993. *Imaginization.* Newberry Park, CA: Sage Publications.

Morgan, G. 2006. *Images of Organizations.* Thousand Oaks, CA: Sage Publications.

Nonaka, I. and H. Takeuchi. 1995. *The Knowledge Creating Company: How Japanese Companies Create the Dynamics of Innovation.* New York: Oxford University Press.

Office of Legislative Counsel. 2010. Patient Protection and Affordable Care Act Health-Related Portions of the Health Care and Education Reconciliation Act of 2010. Available at http://housedocs.house.gov/energycommerce/ppacacon.pdf.

Ohno, T. 1988. *Toyota Production System: Beyond Large-Scale Production.* New York: Productivity Press.

Rosenberg, C. E. 1987. *The Care of Strangers: The Rise of America's Hospital System.* New York: Basic Books, Inc.

Rosenthal, C. 2013. *Big Data in the Age of the Telegraph.* Available at http://www.mckinsey .com/insights/organization/big_data_in_the_age_of_the_telegraph.

Schön, D. A. 1979. Generative metaphor: A perspective on problem-setting in social policy. In *Metaphor and Thought,* edited by A. Ortony, pp. 254–283, Cambridge, UK: Cambridge University Press.

Shewhart, W. A. 1980. *Economic Control of the Quality of Manufactured Product.* Chelsea, MI: Quality Press.

Starr, P. 1982. *The Social Transformation of American Medicine.* New York: Basic Books, Inc.

Starr, P. 2011. *Remedy and Reaction: The Peculiar American Struggle over Health Care Reform.* New Haven, CT: Yale University Press.

Stevens, R. 1999. *In Sickness and in Wealth: American Hospitals in the Twentieth Century.* Baltimore: The Johns Hopkins University Press.

Taylor, F. W. 1911. *The Principles of Scientific Management.* Public Domain Books, Kindle edition, Amazon Digital Services, Inc.

Thomasson, M. 2003. Health Insurance in the United States. EH.net (March). Available at http://eh.net/encyclopedia/health-insurance-in-the-united-states/.

Uhl-Bien, M. 2006. Relational Leadership Theory: Exploring the social process of leadership and organizing. *Leadership Institute Faculty Publications.* Paper 19. Downloaded from and available at http://digitalcommons.unLedu/leadershipfacultypub/19.

Uhl-Bien, M. and B. McKelvey. 2008. Complexity leadership theory: Shifting leadership from the industrial age to the knowledge era. In *Complexity Leadership: Part 1: Conceptual Foundations*, edited by M. Uhl-Bien and R. Marion, pp. 185–224, Charlotte, NC: Information Age Publishing.

US Department of Health and Human Services (DHHS), Centers for Medicare and Medicaid Services. 2012. More than 100,000 health care providers paid for using electronic health records. Available at http://www.businesswire.com/news/home /20120619006144/en/ten0000-health-care-providers-paid-electronic-health.

Wheatley, M. 1992. *Leadership and the New Science: Learning About Organizations from an Orderly Universe.* San Francisco: Berrett-Koehler Publishers.

Womack, J. P., D. T. Jones, and D. Roos. 2007. *The Machine That Changed the World: The Story of Lean Production—Toyota's Secret Weapon in the Global Car Wars That Is Now Revolutionizing World Industry.* New York: Free Press.

Zimmerman, B. 2011. How complexity science is transforming healthcare. In *Sage Handbook of Complexity and Management*, edited by P. Allen, S. Maguire, and B. McKelvey. Thousand Oaks, CA: Sage Publications.

Index

A

Adaptive innovation, *see* Organizational transition (innovation)
Advance-practice nurses, 119
AMA, *see* American Medical Association
American healthcare development, 3–6
    assumptions, 5
    direction, 4
    industrial quality methods, 5
    mental images, 4
    metaphor, 3, 4
    motivation, 5
American Medical Association (AMA), 150

B

Bureaucracy, 45, 153
    display of on organization chart, 100, 162
    financial, 49
    hierarchical structure, 98
    hospital, 39, 48, 105
    layers of, 108
    physicians separated from, 150
    split system, 45
    vertical, 8

C

Cause-and-effect diagram, 56
Centralized innovation, *see* Organizational transition (innovation)
Change agents, 110
Clothing as professional designations, 152
Communication, chain of, 14
Complex system, 8, 82–86, *see also* Organizational transition (structure)
    adaptation and creativity as part of, 166
    adaptive response of employees within, 172

connectivity in, 82
description of, 8
interactions occurring within, 98
organization as, 79, 94
role of leadership within, 35
view of healthcare as, 50
Computers, 17, 132
Consumer health financing, *see* Process transition (financial)
Consumers, patients as, 140
Continuous flow, 29
Continuum of care delivery system, *see* Process transition (delivery system)
Control, *see* Organizational transition (leadership)
Cost controls, juggernaut of, 48
Craftsman model, 115, 152, *see also* Process transition (production method)
Crisis point, 46, 175
Cultural transition (metaphor), 159–168
    flux and transformation metaphor, 160
    healthcare complex adaptive system (21st century), 164–168
        adaptation and creativity, 166
        characteristics, 164
        collaboration, 167
        complex system, 166
        flow of information, 168
        patient-customer interactions, 165
        rules, 165
    levels, 159
    organism metaphor, 160
    processing brain metaphor, 160
    scientific machine (20th century), 161–164
        cause-and-effect image, 162
        characteristics, 161
        control, 163
        departmental structure, 162

181

182 ■ *Index*

employees, machine-like characteristics
of, 161–162
mechanical assumptions, 162
predictability, 162
subtleness, 159
transition assessment charts, 159, 160, 168
Cultural transition (professional), 149–157
assessment chart, 149
difficulty, 149
growth, 150
lobbying, 150
physician autonomy, 150
professional autonomy (20th century),
151–153
characteristics, 151
clothing as professional designations, 152
craftsman model, 152
decision making, 152
hierarchy, 152
indicators of professional status, 153
physician as singular figure, 151
social deference, 153
professional integration (21st century),
154–157
attire, 155
characteristics, 154
decision making, 155
deference, 156
group effectiveness, 156
knowledge sharing, 156
multidisciplinary team, 154
team responsibility, 155
transition assessment charts, 149, 150, 157
Customer, *see* Patient-customer

D

Data collection, 175
Data management, efficiency of, 133
Decision-support software, 39
Deference, 156, 174
Delivery system transition, *see* Process
transition (delivery system)
DMAIC, 57

E

Efficiency
data management, 133
desperate drive to produce, 47
disparity in, 21
hospital, 29
metaphors exemplifying, 100

Electronic information systems
adaptation to effects of, 62
evolution of, 131
transformative benefits of, 135
Emergent relationship, *see* Organizational
transition (relationship)
Employee(s)
acid test for, 94
adaptive response of, 172
burden to purchase care, 48
decision making, 103
experiences shared by, 92
as healthcare consumers, 146
innovations identified by, 36
interaction, 101
machine-like characteristics of, 161–162
negotiations with, 90
serving patient-customers, 34
Employer-sponsored healthcare, 18, 66
Ethical decision, 102

F

Fee-for-service, *see* Process transition (financial)
Financial transition, *see* Process transition
(financial)
Flow, concept of, 29
Flowcharting, 56, 57
Flux and transformation metaphor, 160
Force field analysis, 57
Foreign competition, 21

G

Generative metaphors, 8
Group(s)
assessment of progress, 51
decisions, 116
effectiveness, 156
Guarantees of services, 147

H

Handwritten orders, 14
HCA, *see* Hospital Corporation of America
Healthcare Maintenance Organization Act, 24
Health savings account, 38
Hierarchy, *see* Organizational transition
(structure)
Hospital
bureaucracy, 39
decision making, 152
delivery system (20th century), 124–127

difficulty in applying Six Sigma, 46
dominance of, 125
efficiency, 29
importance of to community, 125
insurance, 143
medical record, 125
medical staff, 45
payment model, 18
reimbursement, 46
role of in creating information
    infrastructure, 129
traditions, 108
20th century image of, 173
Hospital Corporation of America (HCA), 24

I

Industrialization (American healthcare), 21–31
    continuous flow, 29
    control charts, 22
    customer, 25
    delivery of care, 26
    design of services, basis for, 27
    elimination of waste, 28
    flow, concept of, 29
    flowchart image of processes, 29
    foreign competition, 21
    gaining acceptance, 30
    industrialization phase of American
        healthcare, 21
    industrial quality, 24
    Japan's achievements, 23
    Lean methodologies, development of, 24
    Malcolm Baldrige National Quality Award, 23
    Medicare, Conditions of Participation in, 23
    National Demonstration Project, 24
    operational data, monitoring of, 31
    ORYX program, 23
    patient-customer status, recognition of, 27
    primary drivers, 22
    process, structure, and outcome model, 23
    product, search for, 26
    quality efforts, 23
    rapid response to changes, 31
    resistance, 24
    service industry, healthcare as, 22
    Six Sigma, 23, 25, 30
    standardization, 29–30
    Toyota Production System, 23
    value, importance of identifying, 28
    warrior spirit of healthcare, 31
    waste, identification of, 31
    wounded pride, 23

Industrialization (preparing to transition), 43–50
    assumptions, 50
    bureaucracy, 45
    complex system, view of healthcare as, 50
    conflict, 43
    crisis point, 46
    data availability, 50
    emerging images, 44
    employee burden, 48
    hospital medical staff, 45
    hospital reimbursement, 46
    juggernaut of cost controls, 48
    pressures on organizations, 43
    risk models, 48
    Six Sigma, hard part about, 47
Industrialization assessment, 51–58
    cause-and-effect diagram, 56
    DMAIC, 57
    flowcharting, 56
    groups assessing progress, 51
    innovation, 55
    intermediate customers, 53
    lack of transparency, 57
    need for innovation, 55
    patient-customer value, 56
    plan–do–study–act, 57
    process standardization, 54
    project charter, 55
    root cause analysis, 56
    SIPOC, 55, 57
    statistical data analysis, 57
    value stream mapping, 56
    VoC surveys, 57
    walking, 54
    waste elimination, 54
Industry model, 144
Information system transition, *see* Process
    transition (information system)
Innovation transition, *see* Organizational
    transition (innovation)
Insurance
    employer-sponsored, 66
    evolution of, 139
    hospital, 143
    industry, 40
    payment process, 19
    reduction of employer coverage, 18

J

Japan's achievements, 23
JCAH, *see* Joint Commission on Accreditation
    of Hospitals

184 ■ *Index*

Joint Commission on Accreditation
    of Hospitals (JCAH), 23
Just-in-time inventory, 47

K

Knowledge
    employee, 36
    sharing, 115, 156
    system, 131
    tacit, 106

L

Leadership transition, *see* Organizational
    transition (leadership)
Lean
    focus of, 53
    methodologies, development of, 24
    tools and techniques associated with, 55
    waste elimination in, 54
Lobbying, 150

M

McCallum organization chart, 79
Machine image, 39
Malcolm Baldrige National Quality Award, 23
Medicaid, 66
Medical record, coding of, 141
Medicare, 66
    Conditions of Participation in, 23
    deductibles, 38
    rising costs of, 24
Metaphor
    complex system, 8
    efficiency, 100
    flux and transformation, 160
    generative, 8
    organism, 160
    processing brain, 160
    subtleness of, 159
    transition, see Cultural transition (metaphor)
    20th century, 40
Motivation, *see* Signposts and motivation
    to continue journey
Multidisciplinary teams, *see* Process transition
    (production method)

N

Name badges, 36
National Demonstration Project, 24, 46

Negotiations, layers of, 140
Next steps, 175–176
    crisis point, 175
    data collection, 175
    guidance, 176
    industrialization, 175
    transitions appearing, 176
Nurse(s)
    advance-practice, 119
    military style, 105
    orders read by, 14
    -patient interaction, computers and, 136
    progress assessed by, 51
    system, of care created by, 126
    walking, 54

O

Operational data, monitoring of, 31
Organism metaphor, 160
Organizational transition (innovation), 105–113
    adaptive innovation (21st century), 109–113
        change agents, 110
        channeling innovation, 112
        characteristics, 109
        judgment of innovation, 112
        leadership, 109
        problematic innovation, 111
        resources, 111
    centralized innovation (20th century),
        106–109
        characteristics, 106
        hospital traditions, 108
        locked suggestion box, 107
        outside innovation, 107
        point of origin, 107
        positional power, 108, 109
        problematic innovation, 109
        spread of innovation, 107
        vertical lines of power, 107
    tacit knowledge, 106
    transition assessment charts, 106, 113
Organizational transition (leadership), 97–104
    chart, 97
    complex system, interactions occurring
        within, 98
    control (20th century), 98–101
        abuses of power, 99
        efficiency, 100
        employee interaction, 101
        metaphors, 99, 100
        organization charts, 99
        professional power, 100

defining leadership, 98
position power, 97
relational leadership theory, 98
relationships, 98
transition assessment charts, 97, 98, 104
trust (21st century), 101–104
  characteristics, 101
  employee decision making, 103
  employee interaction, 101
  ethical decision, 102
  need for leadership, 103
  new definition of leadership, 104
  problematic responsibility, 103
  redefining leadership, 101
  rules governing operations, 102
Organizational transition (relationship),
      87–95
  complex system, 88
  emergent relationship (21st century), 91–95
    acid test for employees, 94
    characteristics, 91–92
    employee experiences, 92
    job description, 92
    management model, 94
    mission, foundational concepts of, 93
    organizational values, 94
    system cohesion, 93
    work evaluations, 92
  focus, 88
  scientific management, 87
  transactional relationship (20th century),
      89–91
    characteristics, 89
    hierarchical structure, 91
    negotiations, 90
    positional power of management, 90
    tasks, 89
  transition assessment charts, 87, 88, 94
Organizational transition (structure), 77–86
  categories, 79
  complex system (21st century), 82–86
    accountability, shift of, 85
    characteristics, 83
    connectivity, 82
    flow of resources, 84
    information flow, 84
    open structure, 85
    organizational chart, functional
        designations within, 84
    Union and Southern Railway chart, 85
    vertical configuration, 83
  hierarchy (20th century), 79–82
    accountability, 80

allocation of resources, 81
  characteristics, 80
  complex system, 79, 94
  control of activities, 82
  definition, 79
  information flow, 81
  organization chart, 80
  historical background, 78
  McCallum organization chart, 79
  transition assessment charts, 77, 78, 86
ORYX program, 23
Outcomes of care, 145
Outpatient facilities, 16

P

Pareto charts, 57
Path ahead for American healthcare, 7–9
  complex system, 8
  generative metaphors, 8
  industrialization, 7
  metaphor, 8
  relationships, 9
  transition assessment charts, 9
  transition starting point, 8
Patient-customer
  as consumers, 140
  employees serving, 24
  empowerment of, 67
  enculturation of, 14
  expectations of, 40
  flow, 29
  partnership with, 120
  payment, 27
  pertinent, 53
  role of in industrial sense, 28
  status, recognition of, 27
  value (PCV), 56
Patient Protection and Affordable Care Act
      (PPACA), 47
Payment model, 18
PCV, *see* Patient-customer value
PDSA, *see* Plan–do–study–act
Physician
  autonomy, 150
  as center of controversy, 15
  credentialing and licensing of, 23
  as independent craftsman, 115
  order, 14, 141
  -patient interaction, computers and, 136
  rounds, 17
  as singular figure, 151
  system, of care created by, 126

186 ■ *Index*

Plan–do–study–act (PDSA), 57
Positional power, 90, 97, 108
PPACA, *see* Patient Protection and Affordable
    Care Act
Processing brain metaphor, 160
Process transition (delivery system), 123–130
    continuum of care delivery system (21st
        century), 127–130
        characteristics, 127
        configuration, 127
        coordination of care, 128
        links, 128
        network of service agencies, 129
        role of hospitals in creating information
          infrastructure, 129
        urgent care center, 129
    hallmark of 20th century healthcare, 123
    hospital delivery system (20th century),
        124–127
        characteristics, 124
        community quality of life, 125
        customized delivery models, 127
        dominance of hospital, 125
        medical record, 125
        production facility, hospital as, 126
    transition assessment charts, 123,
        124, 130
Process transition (financial), 139–147
    consumer health financing (21st century),
        143–147
        characteristics, 144
        consumer health financing, 144
        employees, 146
        guarantees, 147
        industry model, 144
        obscure process, 144
        outcomes of care, 145
        service delivery system, 144
        transparency of process, 145
    fee-for-service (20th century), 140–143
        characteristics, 140
        hospital insurance, 143
        medical record, coding of, 141
        negotiations, layers of, 140
        outcomes, 142
        physician's order, 141
        uninsured patient, 142
    insurance, 139
    patients as consumers, 140
    payment for healthcare services, 139
    transition assessment charts, 139, 140, 146
Process transition (information system),
    131–138

electronic information systems, evolution
    of, 131
information system isolation (20th century),
    132–135
    characteristics, 132
    computers, introduction of, 132
    data management, efficiency of, 133
    departments needing data processing,
      133
    handwritten record, 132
    inaccessible data, 134
    limitations, 134
information system network (21st century),
    135–138
    characteristics, 135
    connectivity, importance of, 135
    databases, connection of, 137–138
    point of care, 138
    tablet (computer), 136
    technology, 135
system knowledge, 131
transition assessment charts, 131, 132,
    138
Process transition (production method),
    115–122
    changes in processes, 115
    craftsman production (20th century),
      116–119
      care delivery, method of, 118
      characteristics, 116
      emphasis, 116
      expectation, 118
      knowledge of patient details, 117
      perspective, 117
      physician responsibility, 118
      strength of relationships, 117
    group decisions, 116
    independent craftsman, physician as, 115
    multidisciplinary team production (21st
      century), 119–122
      advance-practice nurses, 119
      partnership with patient, 120
      physician's role, 121
      quality of care, 120
      teamwork, 119, 121
    sharing knowledge, 115
    transition assessment charts, 115, 116, 122
Product, search for, 26
Production method transition, *see* Process
    transition (production method)
Professional transition, *see* Cultural transition
    (professional)
Project charter, 55

Q

Quality
    control (industrial), 57
    efforts (20th century), 23
    industrial, 24
    Six Sigma, 30
    variation in, 131

R

RCA, *see* Root cause analysis
Relational leadership theory, 98
Relationship transition, *see* Organizational
    transition (relationship)
Risk models, 48
Root cause analysis (RCA), 56

S

Scientific machine (20th century), 161–164
Second Industrial Revolution, 164
Signposts and motivation to continue journey,
    171–174
    cultural transitions, 174
    deference, 174
    employees, adaptive response of, 172
    financial darkness of 20th century, 173
    hospital, 20th century image of, 173
    industrialization, 174
    multidisciplinary team, 173
    process transitions, 172
SIPOC, 55, 57
Six Sigma, 23, 25
    clinical aspects of care incorporated into, 39
    difficulty of hospitals in applying, 46
    focus of, 53
    hard part about, 47
    quality, 30
    standardization and, 29
    tools and techniques associated with, 55
Social deference, 153
Statistical data analysis, 57
Structure transition, *see* Organizational
    transition (structure)
Suggestion box, 107
System function, leadership as, 35
System knowledge, 131

T

Tablet (computer), 136
Tacit knowledge, 106

ThedaCare, 24
Toyota Production System, 23, 29
Transactional relationship, *see* Organizational
    transition (relationship)
Transition assessment charts, 9
    characteristics, 68
    columns, 72
    cultural transition
        metaphor, 159, 160, 168
        professional, 149, 150, 157
    organizational transition
        innovation, 105, 106, 113
        leadership, 97, 98, 104
        relationship, 87, 88, 94
        structure, 77, 78, 86
    point totals, 71
    process transition
        delivery system, 123, 124, 130
        financial, 139, 140, 146
        information system, 131, 132, 138
        production method, 115, 116, 122
Transition assessment tools, 71–74
    lack of progress, 71
    mapping the transitions, 72, 73
    scorecard, 71, 72, 74
    transitional assessment charts, 71, 73
    transition progress scale, 73, 74
Transition categories and characteristics,
    65–70
    cultural transition group, 68
    delivery system, 68
    financial transition, 68
    industrialization, 65–66
    industrial quality, voluntary implementation
        of, 67
    manufacturing model, 65
    mapping of movement, 69
    metaphorical characteristics, 70
    new demands, 67
    organizational transition group, 68, 69
    origin of categories, 66
    patient-customers, empowerment of, 67
    process transition group, 68, 69
    production method transition, 68
    subtle changes, 69
    transitional assessment charts, 68
    transition categories, 66
Transition groups (organizational, process, and
    cultural), 61–64
    cultural transitions, 63
    delivery system, 63
    electronic information network, 63
    financial transition, 63

188 ■ *Index*

individual transitions, 61
information system transition, 63
innovation transition, 62
kaleidoscope vision, 64
leadership transition, 62
metaphor transition, 63
organizational transitions, 61
process transitions, 62
production method transition, 62
professional transition, 63
relationship transition, 61
structure transition, 61
Trust, *see* Organizational transition (leadership)
20th century American healthcare, 13–20
center of controversy, 15
chain of communication, 14
computers, 17
critical areas, 20
developmental perspective, 13
employer-sponsored healthcare, 18
enculturation of patients, 14
handwritten orders, 14
hospital payment model, 18
hospital privileges, 15
industrialization, challenge of, 13
insurance payment process, 19
outpatient facilities, 16
payment model, 18
physician's order, costs of, 14
system breakdown, 19
21st century American healthcare, 33–40
awards, 36
communication methods, 35–36
decision-support software, 39
discussion groups, 37
drivers of healthcare, 40
employee knowledge, 36
employees serving patient-customers, 34
financing options, 38

health savings account, 38
hospital bureaucracy, 39
industrialization, 40
information system, 35
key metrics, 36
leadership as system function, 35
machine image, 39
Medicare deductibles, 38
metaphors, 40
name badges, 36
patient-customers, expectations of, 40
Six Sigma, 39

U

Uninsured patient, 142
Union and Southern Railway chart, 85
Urgent care center, 129

V

Value
customer definition of, 28
determining, 53
importance of identifying, 28
stream mapping, 56
Vertical bureaucracy, 8
Virginia Mason Medical Center, 24
VoC, *see* Voice of the customer
Voice of the customer (VoC), 53, 57

W

Walking, necessity of, 54
Warrior spirit of healthcare, 31
Waste
elimination, 28, 54
identification of, 31
Work evaluations, 92